MY LOVE WILL KNOW NO BOUNDS

Inspiring Testimonies of Discovering God's Love and Purpose

Through Adoption, Faith, Oppression and Trials

Noreen Weaver

D1411400

WEAVER, MY LOVE WILL KNOW NO BOUNDS

Return, O Israel, to the Lord your God,
for your sins have brought you down.
Bring your confessions, and return to the Lord.
Say to him, "Forgive all our sins and graciously receive us,
so that we may offer you our praises.
Assyria cannot save us, nor can our warhorses.
Never again will we say to the idols we have made
'You are our gods.'
No, in you alone do the orphans find mercy."
The Lord says, "Then I will heal you of your faithlessness;
my love will know no bounds, for my anger will be gone forever.

Hosea 14: 1- 4

AUTHOR'S NOTE

A dear friend once shared with me that if God does things for us and we neglect to share it, we rob Him of the glory due to Him. Over the past twenty three years I have consistently been encouraged, "You need to write a book!" by more people than I can count. In a journal entry from Monday, July 5, 2000, I recorded my first encounter with someone who obviously felt that our Haitian adoption stories alone were worthy of documenting in book form. Unknown to me at the time, he would be the first to encourage these stories to be written;

"Yesterday Pastor asked me if I were getting my notes and journals ready. I asked, 'What for?' He said, 'For your book.' I wonder what that means."

We have been blessed with numerous opportunities to glorify God in sharing our stories of God's divine appointments, and how He has brought precious souls into our family. Telling our stories and witnessing the reactions of those who were listening helped me to realize more fully how powerfully and miraculously God had orchestrated our circumstances.

These pages include the testimonies of my very personal experiences. It is my sincere belief that in His sovereignty, God authored the details of each one therefore it has been difficult for me to accept credit or criticism for the victories or the trials. These stories are my own personal perspectives of the Lord working in my life and through our family. I feel it is an honor, a privilege and a responsibility to share these accounts for the purpose of honoring God for what He has done and also to inspire others to put their faith in action, step out of their own created boundaries and dare to love wherever God leads.

Until my own thinking was challenged while walking out my personal journey of faith, it never occurred to me how highly influenced we have become by all the invisible boxes fallen humanity has built for our Heavenly Father. Color and cultural differences, labels, limiting beliefs, denominational walls, religious worldviews, varying doctrines and beliefs have all been used to distort the lens through which we view our Creator in His love relationship to us and one another. God's plans and purposes for my life have required me to venture beyond various barriers that seemed to be hindering, limiting and restricting God's love. In my desperate search for God, I found Him. God's love cannot be confined or bound by man-made rules, beliefs or conditions.   I have determined that, in following Christ and fully surrendering my life to Him, my love will know no bounds.

All For His Glory,

Noreen Weaver

ABOUT THE AUTHOR

Noreen Weaver is a stay at home wife of forty-two years and mother of fourteen children, of which twelve are now adults. She enjoys and has appreciated the privilege of homeschooling her youngest ten children and is still home educating her two youngest sons. She enjoys Bible studies, gardening, preserving food for her family, lunch dates with friends, and furthering her education through a variety of studies. She is active in Adoption and Foster support groups and has facilitated and mentored many families through adoption. She has studied and received certification in Neuro Linguistics and Cognitive Behavioral Therapy for the purpose of her own personal growth and to help others in pursuing healthy connections in relationships. She adores her two canine friends, Sage and Zahra, and has retired after fifteen years of experience raising quality pets for other families to love. Out of her passion to serve the suffering, she established and directed the former Esther's Voice International, a 501 C 3 organization dedicated to supporting orphans and destitute children in Liberia, Haiti, Uganda, and India. Her efforts continue through financial support in partnership with existing Christian organizations that support orphans and widows

around the world.

ACKNOWLEDGEMENTS

* To my Gracious Savior and Redeemer, my Lord Jesus Christ - I am thankful that you are full of grace and mercy for even a wretch like me. I am thankful that You have taught me and showed me that Your love knows no bounds. I am forever grateful to You for guiding my steps, even when I couldn't always see where You were leading me. May Your name be glorified and honored through the testimonies in this book.

This is for you.

* To My husband, my best friend and confidant - Thank you for patiently enduring through the many battles and trials we have faced together. Thank you for listening to the voice of God and allowing Him to lead you. I love you…. more.

* My mother is gone to be with Jesus now, but I know how excited she would be to know that this book finally got written. She was my greatest supporter in everything I pursued. She taught me some of life's most valuable lessons. She loved me unconditionally.

* To my much loved and cherished children that were conceived in my heart - You now have a written account of how God has worked in each of your lives. I trust that you will each continue on your own

faith journey and honor God with all your hearts and all your souls and all your lives. Don't be afraid to be vulnerable and let your faith be tested. The Lord has incredible plans and purposes for each one of you.

* Thank You ZoAnn Wolfe, Grace Weaver, Addie Weaver, Ian Weaver, Jan Close, Chad and Christy Zaucha, Catherine Matthys, Mari Graham, Evelyn Rexford, Sarah Ruetz and Elsie Weaver for your prayers, words of encouragement and your help and support in every way.

* I am sincerely thankful for each one who encouraged me to write this book over the years.

WEAVER, MY LOVE WILL KNOW NO BOUNDS

"Store up for yourselves treasures above

where rust and moth do not destroy."

Matthew 16:19-20

Proceeds from the sale of this book will be shared in support of:

Haiti Clean Water

Asia Harvest

World Orphans

Real Hope for Haiti

The Least of These (Widow and Orphan support- Tanzania)

Wee Lambs Adoption Fund Assistance

TABLE OF CONTENTS

Chapter 1

My Father's Daughter

"God decided in advance to adopt us into his own family by

bringing us to himself through Jesus Christ.

This is what He wanted to do and it gave Him great pleasure.

So we praise God for the glorious grace He has poured out on us

who belong to his dear Son.

He is so rich in kindness and grace that he purchased our freedom

with the blood of His Son and forgave our sins."

Ephesians 1:5-6

"You ain't never gonna amount to nothin." His voice was

stern and harsh as he freely made known his bleak perspective of my

future. I don't remember how many times I heard it. Maybe it was actually just that one painful, unforgettable time, nevertheless, I grew up knowing my dad's expectations of me seemed less than promising. As a young adolescent girl, I didn't know at the time that I could have and should have rejected his unfair predictions. My identity was warped by an emotionally immature and distant alcoholic father. As a result I suffered for most of my childhood and into my adulthood with what most people would refer to now as "low self-esteem".

I didn't grow up in a Christian home. The only evidence of God in our home was displayed on my mother's bedroom dresser. I remember clearly her specific instructions on how I should carefully dust the top of her black leather Bible with the large gold cross embossed on the front, but I was never to lay anything on top of it. I had no idea what was so special about that book, or why she respected its external presence. I had never seen her open it, but I knew it must have had some significance to my mother for some reason. My mom became a Christian when she was fifteen years old. That was her story as I understood it. She led her parents to Christ and her family began attending a Nazarene church. I don't have an understanding of what happened after that, but sometime after her impartial first and only year of college, my mom met my

dad and they married. I'm pretty sure God was never a welcome

partner in their marriage. The only glimpses I had ever witnessed of

God's love were infrequent precious times spent with my maternal

grandparents and my summer visits with my mom's sister, Aunt Jan

and my Uncle Ralph, and their four sons, who were slightly younger

than me. I always knew they possessed something we were

definitely missing. I know they must have prayed for me. They

were the only real Christian influences in my first eighteen years of

life. When my grandparents came to visit, the atmosphere in our

house seemed to change drastically. There was a strange contrast

between the peacefulness in their presence and my dad's obvious

discomfort over his forced change of conduct. All cuss words, mean

remarks and arguments between my parents were intentionally put

on hold during their rare visits to our home.

While growing up in the Great Lake State of Michigan, my

parents owned and operated a successful excavating business in the

middle of the mitten. My dad taught us a strong work ethic. It

seemed there was always work to be done; garden weeds to be

pulled, vegetables to be preserved for winter, wood to be stacked, eggs to gather and animals to feed and water. Daylight meant

activity. My dad worked from sun up to sun down and he expected

the same from us. Sunday mornings were for polka music on the

record player and on weekends, the four of us children played in a

country music family band. My dad loved country music. He

encouraged musical talent and provided my older siblings with

music lessons. We performed at festivals, taverns, holiday parties,

and wedding receptions. My oldest sister played the accordion and

my other sister and my brother played the guitar. A hired friend,

Gary, played the drums. I was the youngest of four children. At

three years old, long before I ever understood the meaning of the

words to the songs, I sang, "Your Cheatin Heart" by Hank Williams,

"You Ain't Woman Enough" by Loretta Lynn and "I Don't Wanna

Play House" by Tammy Wynette while standing on a metal folding

chair so I could be seen by the crowd. I was nine years old when my

oldest sister moved away to attend college. That was the end of our

little family band and I missed those opportunities to sing which was

the one thing I seemed to be able to do well enough to please my

dad.

I have always loved children. By the time I was twelve years old, I had started babysitting for my cousin's one year old little girl. As a teenager, I became a frequent sitter among our rural neighbors. I enjoyed babysitting and my weekends were usually booked. One close neighbor, a young mother of two little boys that I frequently babysat for, thought that I would be a perfect match for her youngest brother. She seemed proud of the fact that he was a seventeen year old high school football player and was sure I would be impressed with that status as well. Sure enough, we started dating just after we met. I was just fifteen years old that summer of 1978. Todd became my husband just three years later when I was one week shy of my nineteenth birthday. I was first drawn to Todd because of the way he interacted and connected with his two young nephews. I saw potential in this young man that seemed to have the capability to love children just as I did.

Prior to getting married, I had started attending a small country Baptist church just outside of town with my cousin, who was also my best friend growing up. This was where I had my first real encounter with the Holy Spirit. This is where I learned of my need for salvation. This was where I experienced being born again and where I was baptized. I know some people don't have dramatic conversion experiences, especially those who have been exposed to a knowledge of God all their lives, but for me, my conversion was an unforgettable moment in time. Something wonderful, indescribable and supernaturally significant happened in my life that day. I felt a newness of life realizing what God had done for me. It was as if my Heavenly Father reached out to me and made Himself known to me through His abiding presence. It was a once in a lifetime experience I will treasure all the days of my life. Little did I know the long pilgrimage yet to come. Although I had experienced a love like I'd never known when I received Jesus as my Savior, and became the daughter of the King of Kings, it was just the beginning of a lifelong, progressive, and ongoing transformation that resulted in many blessings and trials.

"But to all who believed him and accepted him,
He gave the right to become children of God.
They were reborn - not with a physical birth
resulting from human passion or plan –
but a birth that comes from God."

John 1:12-13

As naive as I was about the scriptures, I knew enough to know that I could not be married to, or unequally yoked with an unbeliever so I shared my newfound faith with my boyfriend, Todd. At first, I wasn't quite sure if he was just chasing after me or truly chasing after God at that point, but he did give his life to Christ and he did follow through with baptism as a symbol of his commitment to dying to self, and confessing Jesus as Lord. After we were married in August of 1981, we soon fell away and backslid into old patterns having no spiritual foundation, or any close Christian family or strong Christian friends our age to encourage us and help us grow.

A few years later, when our oldest daughter started preschool, I met another mom who had become a good friend and she invited us to attend their church. Off and on over the next fourteen years, we made that church our home and we started growing in our knowledge and understanding of God as we began walking in relationship to Him. My pre-school mom friend and her sister and I started singing together as a praise and worship team. We sang at our church, other churches and ladies retreats. My favorite songs to sing were the old hymns such as "Washed in the

Blood", and contemporary songs such as, "Crucified with Christ" by

Philips Craig and Dean. These messages were in direct contrast to

the songs I had sung publicly over thirty years prior. Instead of

singing to please my earthly father, I now was singing to honor my

Heavenly Father. Only now, I perfectly understood and embraced

every message in every song I sang.

Our wedding Day August 28, 1981

Chapter 2

Divine Inspiration

"When you became a Christian, you were immediately adopted

as a child of the heavenly king.

The King's business became your business.

And now as your Savior and Lord,

Christ wants to bring your life into the middle of His activity…"

(Experiencing God, Revised and Expanded

by Henry and Richard Blackaby, page 2)

In the early summer of 1996, I read a book that profoundly

changed my perspective on Christian living. It was titled,

"Experiencing God: Knowing and Doing the Will of God" by Henry

Blackaby. The overall message in the book encouraged me to "Look to see where God was working and join Him there". This central theme of the book changed my life forever. Little did I realize while I was reading it that the Lord was arranging an important assignment for us that would change our family dynamics in profound and numerous ways. Through a progression of opportunities and circumstances, divine appointments and testing, our spiritual growth and our faith were about to increase.

It had been quite a busy summer. I had been helping take care of my seventy two year old mother-in-law who was nearing the end of her battle with congestive heart failure. I took every opportunity to pray with her, hoping that she would surrender her heart to the Lord before she passed away. Prior to her death in June, we had been challenged during a church service to share the love of Christ by opening our homes and hosting a high school student from Kazakhstan for a few weeks. Our church had been sponsoring a Christian school there and the goal was to immerse these students in American culture while also showing them the love of Christ in a Christian home setting. These students were children of wealthy dignitaries. In their Christian school they had been taught scriptures by memory and were exposed to the gospel but they had no understanding of what it was like to live out the Christian faith and abide in Christ as a follower. We were assigned a 14 year old girl named Olga (pronounced Ol-ya).

After my mother-in-law's funeral in June, I was feeling too overwhelmed and too emotionally exhausted to even consider getting our home ready and entertaining another teenager in addition to the four children we had at home; then ages 16yrs - 9yrs. I shared with a friend one day my thoughts of surrendering our commitment to host Olga and mentioned that I had been considering finding another family for her to stay with. Without hesitation, she quickly encouraged me to not back out of the arrangement and even offered to help me get my house ready for our visitor from the other side of the globe. I will never forget her words to me: "You might miss a big blessing if you don't take her." I'm sure my dear friend never realized the enormity of the truth in the statement she had made, but the Lord used her words to inspire me to go for it and prepare for our young house guest, not realizing the tremendous life changing impact she was about to leave with us.

Olga came and spent the most part of August 1996 with our family. We took her to McDonalds, we took her to big shopping centers and we took her to church and family church camp, all of which were brand new experiences for her. We fell in love with this sweet, respectful girl although communicating wasn't always easy. She could speak limited English, but she seemed to understand more than she could speak. This proved to be especially hard when it came time for her to leave us and travel back to her family in Kazakhstan. The day we were preparing to take her back to the airport, there were no words, just much weeping and many tears coming from Olga. I asked her several times, "What's wrong?" I knew she loved her family very much and they were a very close knit family so I thought she would be happy to be going home. Two weeks after her return, I got an eye opening letter from Olga in the mail. She must have written it soon after her plane touched the ground, or possibly on her long flight across the Atlantic Ocean. In the letter, she expressed her heart in written words that she could not express verbally before she left. In a few words, she wanted me to know that our relationships were not like their relationships. I immediately surmised that it was the love of Christ in our home that Olga knew she was going to miss. My heart was somehow encouraged to think we had actually made that much of an impact on her life in the short time she was with us.

It didn't take long for God to turn this experience into an amazing invitation while awakening a passion in my heart that I didn't even know existed.

Olga kept in touch with us through letters for many years as she went through her studies at The Hebrew University of Jerusalem and Portland State University.   She is now married and is a mother of two sons. They live in the state of Oregon. We now keep in touch primarily through social media.

Of all the divine encounters I've experienced over the years, meeting Olga was certainly the most profound. She not only made a difference in my life, but she inspired us to reach out to help change the lives of many others as well.

Olga- 14 years old, August 1996

Chapter 3

A Little Hope

"Never be afraid to trust an unknown future to a known God."

Corrie Ten Boom

It took a lot of courage for me to approach my husband with the idea. I knew God had placed an urging in my heart, but I feared Todd would immediately reject it since it was quite a stretch even for my own imagination. But just maybe….. just maybe, if we had the capacity to fall in love with Olga like we did and to take care of Olga like we did and make an impact on her life like we did, then just maybe we had the capacity to love an orphan who had no family, no parents, no home and no one to call their own.

Todd responded in a half-hearted laugh at my crazy idea but it didn't take long for him to realize that I wasn't joking, I was serious. Thankfully he entertained all my conversations and didn't immediately reject them. Soon we both found ourselves seriously considering adopting from Central America. I contacted Children's Hope, a local adoption agency, and they agreed to send us the preliminary adoption application for our home study paperwork. Coincidentally, this agency specialized in Central American adoptions. They had contacts in Guatemala and Honduras.

Walking out of my comfort zone was hard, yet exciting for me. It seemed my life was always defined by the opinions of others and now God was calling us to do something that I never dared to dream or had ever hoped or believed was possible. In my limited understanding, only wealthy people who couldn't have biological children adopted children. It was such a foreign idea to me that it was obviously not "my" idea at all, but God's.

As we began praying about this tugging at our hearts to adopt an orphan, I resigned to the understanding that God had initiated this adoption so therefore He would give us whatever child He wanted us to have. For reasons unknown to me, we both seemed to agree, maybe because of Olga, that we wanted to adopt a girl. A baby girl, "we decided", under two years old would be the request

we would soon specify on our home study application.

The presence of God in our adoption pursuit was so strong

that we never thought to ask for human guidance or opinions. God

was giving us a baby! Asking our family or our Pastor for

permission to adopt was, for me, the same as asking their permission

to keep a baby we had physically conceived. Aborting this adoption

God had conceived in our hearts was not an option, no matter who

might disapprove. Little did we know of the resistance soon to

come.

God was about to stretch our faith in ways we had never imagined.

Looking at the requirements for Central America was a little

overwhelming, especially the financial part. We soon discovered

that adoptions through an attorney in Central America at that time

were requiring an astronomical amount of money. I recalled an

acquaintance that I had met at a Women's Bible Study. I

remembered that she and her husband had adopted two baby boys

from Haiti the year before. While Todd was at work one day, I

looked up her number and called her. She was very supportive and

gave me all the contact information to the orphanage they had adopted from along with a brief overview of what they required to get started with the process. The Haitian adoption fees were a mere fraction of what was required for Guatemala or Honduras. This seemed to be a more realistic avenue for us! I was really feeling excited and couldn't wait to share with Todd what I had found out. When he came home from work, I told him about this new potential adoption opportunity. Neither of us barely even knew where Haiti was on a map, but one thing was for certain, Todd did NOT think that bringing a black child into an all white family was such a good idea. He knew that there were racial prejudices on both sides of our families and he did not think it would be fair to the child. I was a bit hurt by his negativity, but as we went to bed that night I prayed silently. "Lord, it is not my job to change my husband's mind or his heart. If this is Your will then Lord You will have to do a work in him by the power of Your Holy Spirit. Lord, I will not beg or plead or argue with him over this. I surrender to Your will and I will respect my husband's decision." After a long night of literally wrestling with God, (as Todd himself describes it now) he got up and went to work as usual. I continued to pray throughout the day for God to show us His will. As soon as Todd stepped into the house after work later that day the first thing he said to me was, "Haiti huh?" The Lord had very rapidly answered my very specific prayer and Todd was now willing to at least consider a Haitian adoption in spite of his valid concerns.

It didn't take long before we found out that not everyone was as excited as we were about what God was doing in our lives. We asked to meet with our Pastor about what we felt God was showing us. He thought maybe we should try sponsoring an orphan rather than going to the "extreme" of bringing one into our home. It seemed he perceived what we felt was a calling as something unattainable. A few friends felt that we had enough children of our own and we didn't "need" any more. When my dad found out we were adopting a child, his comment was, "I sure hope it ain't BLACK!" I gained a personal perspective of what Jesus was saying when He warned us not to cast something precious before those who would not understand its value.

One of the biggest hurts came when my best friend shared with another friend that we were just doing this for "attention". We quickly learned:

"If you are ever tempted to look for outside approval,

realize that you have compromised your integrity."

(Epictetus)

God had created just enough confidence in me that I could say, "I am willing to be a fool for Jesus Christ." I am willing to follow Him on this journey into the unknown no matter how lonely it might get or how foolish it might seem to those who were watching. I determined to trust Him to lead and guide us, no matter what the outcome might be. We knew that we were not perfect parents or perfect Christians, but we were willing to be used by God for His purposes if it were "His" will. We did not have any solid assurance that we would ever get approved for adoption but a faith beyond ourselves was calling us to press forward into the unchartered territory of many unknowns.

It was a major test of faith to dive into an international adoption without the funds to support it. Todd had a decent, secure job and we had a nice home, but that was it. As hard as we tried to fundraise, nothing seemed to work. Yet in spite of our feeble efforts, God somehow provided at every single turn. It never came in a lump sum, but as we needed it, God somehow provided. This experience created a newfound dependence on God for all our needs as we learned to know and trust Him more and more as Jehovah

Jireh, our faithful provider.

One of our biggest challenges during our first adoption came

when the FBI lost my fingerprints. This set us back for a couple of

months and forced us to trust God in the timing. After several

weeks, it was suggested by our social worker that I have my prints

retaken and resubmit them. One day I was sharing with a friend

about my conversations with Connie S. at the Federal Bureau of

Investigations regarding our situation. I was desperate to find a

person to talk to that cared enough to listen to my serious problem. I

remember my best friend's mother, Betty, saying, "Noreen! Shy,

timid Noreen? YOU called the FBI?" Desperate measures call for

desperate actions! Until then, I never realized that God had the

ability to give me courage beyond what I ever dreamed I was

capable of.

Jeremiah 29:11 became very special to me. God was

unfolding some big plans. He was planning to give a precious little

girl "a hope and a future" and He was choosing US to be an

important part of her life! As the Lord was speaking what seemed

like volumes to urge us in the beginning of our journey, I found it necessary to journal. All my entries started with "Dear Hope," as we had begun to call our unknown daughter. September became a blur and October was upon us; things were moving fast. So much had happened since Olga's August visit from Kazakhstan. One day I felt inspired to pray for what I believed to be an unborn baby girl and her biological mother.

- October 19, 1996 journal entry:

Dear Hope,

The Lord has been speaking loudly to me through the scriptures. What precious peace and comfort He gives me through His word. I have been strengthened and encouraged over and over again. He knows exactly what to tell me when I need to hear it. I have been invited by a Pastor from a neighboring church to sing at a Memorial Service for those in the community that have died and gone on to heaven. If your natural mother dies, Hope, I want you to know that I am praying that she will come to know the Lord before she does so that one day we can all be united as family in heaven.

As days went by, more journal entries included our steps in preparing for our little gift from God:

- October 21, 1996 - We sent out our applications to the adoption agency and our biographies and application to the orphanage in Haiti.

- October 24, 1996 - Todd put the crib together!

Then, just one month later....

- November 24, 1996, two letters came in the mail from Don and Doris Peavey, Directors of Ebenezer Glenn Orphanage in Haiti. The first letter explained that we were accepted as adoptive parents and informed us that they did not have any baby girls but that they had a lot of little boys that needed loving Christian homes too! This second letter was attached to the first;

"Before the mail went out today, a baby girl came in weighing three pounds. She has sores in her mouth from unsterile nipples. They had been feeding her sugar water to keep her alive. We are unsure if she will make it; her mother died after giving birth. Her name is Adeline Monimet. She is yours if you will have her."

Oh the elation and thrill of our hearts! It was as if we had just given birth! We began asking everyone and anyone who would to pray for our tiny Haitian baby girl. Her circumstances were so bleak yet by faith we believed with all of our hearts that she would survive and thrive. She was physically so very far away yet so close and so tangible to our hearts.

We were told her name was Adeline (pronounced Adelyn), the name her mother had given her before she died. It was two long months later, in January of 1997, before we heard anything again. Along with our first photo, Doris wrote this note:

Dear Noreen,

12/12/96

How special to see how God is working. By all visible signs she should be dead. Now I realize with all the prayers that are going up for the tiny bundle, why she is still living……..

Adeline Monimet Hope- 2 months old

Social / Medical Statement for Adeline Monimet

January 1997

Adeline Monimet was brought to Ebenezer Glenn Orphanage by her father on Friday, November 15, 1996. She was born November 4, 1996 in Laborque, Haiti. Her mother died after a long illness with a high fever (no doubt malaria) after the birth of Adeline. Adeline was the eighth child to her parents. At the time of her arrival at the orphanage, she weighed three pounds, zero ounces. She was premature and malnourished. Formula was given to her from a bottle but she would not suck. Upon examination, a small open sore was discovered under her tongue, probably from unsterile nipples. It was treated and repeated attempts were made to get her to drink. It was questionable if she would survive. After considering placing a feeding tube down her, the attempt was made to get her to suck. She did begin to take small amounts at a time and it appeared she would survive. She required twenty four hour care and was fed frequently through the day and night. A nursing mother at the orphanage breast fed her because she had begun suffering from diarrhea. The breast milk was tolerated better than the formula but the breast milk and formula was alternated as this mother was feeding two other babies. At eight weeks of age, Adeline weighed five pounds and four ounces. She adjusted well to the formula and the diarrhea diminished. At this time, Adeline appears to be in good stable condition. She is eating well and gaining weight rapidly. She is bright, alert and seems to respond favorably to stimuli. Her chances for living a normal life are expected to be excellent.

Six long months passed as we learned many valuable lessons in how faith grows through trials. Corrie Ten Boom once said, "Faith sees the invisible, believes the unbelievable and receives the impossible."

On June 9, 1997, I met and held Adelyn Monimet Hope Weaver for the first time. I did not apologize and I was not embarrassed by the flood of tears as I repeatedly whispered, "Thank you Jesus, Thank You Jesus, Thank You Jesus." Oh how sweet was the victory. I had never experienced the depth of Christ's love like I did at that moment.

Don and Doris Peavey, founders and directors of Ebenezer Glenn Orphanage in Desselines, Haiti had escorted our precious new daughter home for us from Haiti. It became a great pleasure to get to know these giants in the faith. They became spiritual mentors to Todd and me over the years to come. They visited our home several times and we loved them dearly.

Don and Doris Peavey with Adelyn, June 9, 1997

Adelyn appeared to have been well taken care of. Other than being very small for her age, she was healthy. She weighed just 13 pounds at her seven month well check and wore a size 3 months in baby clothing. She was a very happy, content and trusting baby. She acted as if she had always been with us. Her adjustment was super easy. We all catered to her and adored her immensely! She smiled and giggled with glee at every bit of attention she received, which was a lot with four much older brothers and sisters! She was such a joy! With her bubbly little personality, she seemed to draw attention everywhere we went. We were so happy and so proud of

our adorable gift from God. We couldn't have loved her more if she

had been born to us.

Baby Adelyn – 13 months old

Chapter 4

Over The Rainbow

Then God said, "I am giving you a sign of my covenant with you..."

Genesis 9:12

It was quite exciting to find out that my niece who had been attending Taylor University was planning on going to Haiti for a solo mission trip. I suggested to Todd that possibly we could accompany her on her journey and go on to visit the orphanage where Adelyn was from. He readily agreed as Don and Doris Peavey, Directors of Ebenezer Glenn Orphanage had previously invited him to come and work on their church building project. We scheduled ticket arrangements for flights with Missionary Flights International which was then based in Fort Lauderdale, Florida. Our trip was scheduled for January 5, 1999. Since we had several boxes

of supplies we had collected for the orphanage, we drove a rental car

to Fort Lauderdale and checked in our several tubs and boxes of

supplies with MFI the day prior to our flight. We had made

arrangements for our children to stay with family members and felt

good about knowing they would be in great hands while we were

gone. Everything seemed to easily fall into place. In the midst of a

winter snowstorm we drove from Michigan to Florida with several

hundred pounds of donated supplies for the orphanage in tow. When

we arrived at MFI the day of our departure, we were given a

message from Don and Doris. They would not be available to travel

to pick us up in Cap Haitien where we would be landing so they had

arranged for us to stay and work with another missionary couple that

was returning to Haiti on our same flight.

It was my first experience riding in an old retired military

plane that seated about 12 people. After briefly having landed to

refuel in Jamaica, we looked intently out our windows as we began

our descent into Haiti. As we flew closer and closer toward the

tropical island, I was in awe of the contrast between the beauty of the

mountainous countryside and the obvious poverty of the people.

Smoke billowed heavenward as cooking fires dotted the rugged mountainsides. Todd gently bumped me with his elbow to get my attention and pointed out his window. I looked and saw that we were flying over the top of a beautiful, full rainbow. "A sign of a promise", I thought out loud to myself. I had never seen a rainbow from above. It was an amazing sight as we got a full view from the top of the arch. I wondered what all God had in store for us in this visit to our daughter Adelyn's homeland as I repeated to myself over and over, "A sign of a promise". For some unknown reason, I felt as if there was some great significance in that rainbow.

Haiti was everything I expected and more. Poverty abounded and the smell was truly offensive. After working alongside our new missionary friends for a couple of days, Don and Doris arrived to pick us up. The four hour road trip from Cap Haitien to Dessalines was quite interesting. Our stop at a primitive gas station provided me with my first encounter with a begging child. It was recommended that we didn't start handing out money or food due to the fact that we could be bombarded with aggressive mobs looking for their share. Doris Peavey, the orphanage director from Ebenezer Glenn Orphanage, must have seen the compassion in my eyes for an obviously malnourished little boy with orange nappy hair and red, bloodshot eyes. She gave me permission to give him my remaining icy cold Coke just as we were leaving. Even though it had no nutritional value, the little boy was absolutely thrilled with my meager gift and immediately guzzled down the only token of love I was allowed to share.

For the next few days we acclimated to the hot dry weather. In spite of the abundance of mosquitoes, geckos and tarantulas, I fell in love with Haiti and especially its people. At the guesthouse, I cooked and laundered clothing by hand for Todd, myself and two other men that were there to work on the church building at the orphanage. Communicating with the children at the orphanage was quite a challenge since I knew very little to no Creole. While looking out the kitchen window while doing dishes each day I would pray, "Father what is my purpose here?" I continually kept seeking the Lord. For some reason I felt as if we had yet to discover the reason for which we were really there. I sensed that God had a grander purpose in my being there than merely tending to dirty dishes, dirty laundry and attempting to mend clothes for the children with my limited sewing skills. One day, one of the young boys brought me little eight month old Markie, a baby we had been sponsoring. I had fun playing with him and taking care of him for the afternoon. He smiled when I spoke to him and didn't seem to care that I was speaking a foreign language. Then one of the older girls brought me his supper for me to feed to him. I didn't immediately notice the contents of his little bowl, but I soon realized that this normally small task for this seasoned mother was going to require more bravery than I believed I possessed at the time. "Lord, help me," I prayed as I maneuvered the spoon between the tiny squirming maggots and the small white particles of rice.

One Sunday we all assembled at the little chapel on the orphanage compound and crowded in as we sat on old primitive wooden benches. It seemed everyone over twelve years old was holding an infant or a toddler on their lap. It was steaming hot and I didn't understand a word that the Pastor said, but I was so moved by the powerful sermon and the worship singing that I couldn't hold back my emotions! Thankfully my tears mingled with the sweat dripping off my face, so it wasn't too obvious that I was overwhelmed by the experience. As we walked away from one of the most memorable church services I've ever attended, I decided to go sit in the shade in front of the baby dormitory, feeling incredibly

full and overflowing with the love of God. I tried to communicate

with some of the older girls as they set about changing the little ones

out of their good Sunday best and into their play clothes. I held a

toddler on my lap and we both enjoyed a good cuddle. To my

surprise, Doris came to me and asked, "Would you like two more?"

I had no idea what she was talking about and must have had a very

confused look on my face, as she pointed to the driveway where I

saw in the near distance a small statured Haitian man and a thin

teenage girl holding what looked like a lump of rags in each of their

arms. She explained that this man had brought in his newborn twins.

Their mother had died after they were born and there was no way for

him to feed the babies. He said he had thirteen other children and he

could not take care of them. Doris explained that if they did not take

them that she knew they would die, but they were shorthanded and

didn't have enough workers to take care of two more newborn

infants. I knew that it was not my place to interfere with their

business, but as the Haitian Directors got together to make a decision

about whether to keep them or turn them away, I silently begged

God not to let them go.

My heart fluttered while my mind raced back to a recent

time. A couple of months earlier, we had received a call from an

American missionary Pastor who had been serving in Haiti. He

asked if we would be willing to take newborn twins. We had started

entertaining thoughts of another adoption since our first experience

was such a huge blessing to our family. We fasted and prayed and

"YES!" We would be glad to take newborn twins. I had shared my

heart with Todd and said, "If I ever had twins, I would want boy/girl

twins. Sure enough, the Pastor was asking us to take boy/girl twins!

We prayed for them and sent them formula and other supplies while

the Pastor attempted to gather their documents. But before we ever

got too far into the process of adoption, an Uncle stepped forward to

take the orphaned infants. We were a bit sad, but quickly submitted

to God's will for them and were thankful that they had relatives

willing to care for them.

I quickly reminded Doris that I was available to take care of

the babies for the remainder of our stay so she could take that bit of

information into their meeting to help with their decision. When

she returned, she invited me to go with her as she approached the

father, who was holding one of the infants. She pulled away a worn out, filthy red floor rug that covered the naked baby boy. I looked

in the teenage girl's arms and there was the smaller twin, a baby girl

wrapped in a filthy, formerly white piece of unrecognizable clothing.

I silently reminded the Lord as if He didn't already know our

purpose in being there, "LORD! Boy/girl twins, the desire of my

heart!!"

Doris required the father to sign some documents of

relinquishment that would grant them legal permission to keep the

babies at the orphanage. After some further information was

gathered from the father, we took the babies to feed and bathe them

at the main house. In my limited understanding, I would have been

quick to feed the babies first, believing nourishment to be their

greatest need at the time, but I quickly learned through Doris'

wisdom that they needed a bath first, since tetanus was a big threat to

these filthy little precious ones. There was black soot in their noses

and ears from the coal fires used for cooking inside the dirt floor hut

where they were born. We removed the thin strips of dirty white

rags that were safety pinned across their mid- section, covering their

umbilical cords. It was explained to me that it was some sort of a

voodoo ritual that was believed to keep evil spirits from entering the baby's body. Doris went to the storage room to hunt for some

newborn clothing, bottles, diapers and whatever she could find. To

my surprise she came out with handmade pink flannel rosebud cloth

diapers that my sister-in-law had made and we had sent for our 3

pound little Adelyn over two years previously. She had found a

couple of small outfits, a baby quilt, some scraps of cloth for diapers

and diaper pins. She also found two four ounce bottles and some

powdered formula. We were all set except for lacking diaper

coverings. Living in Haiti for over 30 years as a missionary, Doris

was an expert in the "making due with what you have" department.

She suggested we take a couple of quart size freezer bags that we

had brought along with the supplies and cut two holes in the bottom

corners of each one, making the holes just big enough for each little

leg. It actually worked quite well!

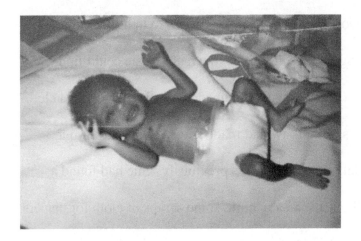

Four pound Baby Girl in her quart size Ziploc bag

At their first initial weigh in, the baby boy weighed five pounds and the baby girl weighed four pounds. I took my foster mother job very seriously while continually reminding myself that I was working for the Lord at this orphanage and these babies would not be going home with us. How do you detach yourself from newborn motherless babies? Impossible - for me anyway. At the guesthouse, we made a little bed of thick quilts and blankets on the floor beside my side of our bed for the twins. To make matters worse for me, throughout the next few days, Todd made several trips from his job doing electric wiring on the tabernacle across the yard of the orphanage compound to the guesthouse to check on the babies! It was one thing for me to be easily attached to these infants, but to watch my husband form such a quick attachment was another

story! My daily chores now included hand washing baby diapers,

regular feedings, bathing and regular weigh-ins at the clinic to make

sure they were growing and gaining weight.

One day I took the babies to the main house for a visit. Out

of the blue, Doris asked me if I felt that God wanted us to adopt

these babies. I was quite excited by the thought of it. I admired and

looked up to Doris as a solid Spirit led Christian. She wasn't one to

be led by emotion, so her inquiry was especially interesting to me.

Then she asked, "What day did you fly into Haiti?" I quickly

replied, "The fifth". "That was the day they were born," she

reported. My mind flashed back to the rainbow. "A sign of a

promise." In my imagination, it seemed quite possible that these

twins were born under that rainbow visible from our airplane

window the day we had arrived! I could hardly contain the joy! I

said to Doris, "It must be a sign!" "We aren't supposed to look for

signs," she said. "Must be a coincidence then," I countered,

somewhat sarcastically. She smiled knowing that we both knew

there is no such thing as a coincidence as a believer in God. I'm sure

Doris and I agreed that coincidences are simply God's way of remaining anonymous. To me, they are like the fingerprints of God touching upon our life's circumstances, showing us He is right there seeing and overseeing every detail of our lives, encouraging us along the way.

Todd and I began allowing ourselves to fully express our love for the twins believing in our hearts that the Lord had intended for us to adopt them before they were even born. Now my purpose in being there made perfect sense!

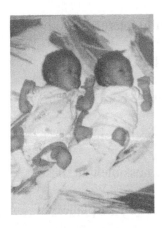

Newborn Twins- Ebenezer Glenn Orphanage- Desselines, Haiti
January 1999

Doris made it clear that they were not doing adoptions any longer. She said they were getting too old to make the additional trips into Port-AuPrince to meet with the attorney and collect documents so if we wanted to adopt the twins we would have to find another orphanage that would keep them and do the paperwork on the Haiti end for us before we left the country. I was lost. We knew no one else in Haiti and had no access to a vehicle, phone, computer or any other possible way to communicate with anyone outside the orphanage walls.

It was inevitable that our time to leave Haiti would eventually come after our short ten day visit and we still had no one to take the twins and complete our adoption. We were forced to hand over the babies to the young teenage girls who were in charge of the baby dormitory and say good-bye not knowing for sure if or when we would ever again see the twins we had grown to love. As our van traveled over the rough, dusty dirt roads from Dessalines back to Port-au-Prince to catch our flight, I sobbed uncontrollably. As I took in the distant mountainous scenery from the van window, my internal conversation with God went something like this:

"Did you really bring me here just to break my heart? Lord you MADE these mountains. Your word says you have the power to MOVE mountains. Please help us arrange the adoption of our twins." By the time we arrived in Port, I had finally stopped sobbing. I was numb from crying and had no choice but to surrender to my desperate circumstances. Don made a stop at a lumber yard to

order some lumber and other building materials and Doris said she

was going to make a phone call while we waited in the van. Several

minutes later, Doris came to the van and shared the reason for her

call. She had called Gladys Sylvestre, the Director from The

RAINBOW of Love Orphanage right there in Port-au-Prince!

Arrangements would be made for the twins to be transferred into

Gladys' care and she agreed to complete our adoptions for us! I

listened with less than a half of an ear as Doris went on to share her

concerns and said something about that orphanage's good points and

not so good points. At the moment I was only interested in the fact

that God was promising to finish what He started! With chills down

my spine, and Holy Spirit goose bumps across my arms, I looked at

Todd in disbelief. "The RAINBOW OF LOVE Orphanage?!" God's

confirmation of His promise to me on the day they were born.

Getting on the plane to return home wasn't so difficult now since I

knew that in a few months I would be returning to bring our forever

blessings home.

With a joyful peace, we boarded our plane for home. My

focus shifted to entertaining thoughts of considering names for our new son and daughter. The girls at the orphanage had named them Jessy and Jessyka, but we wanted to put more meaning and thought into the names of our tiny new gifts from God. The rainbow was such a big part of their story that we couldn't help but think of "Noah" for our new little man. Doris often referred to Jessyka as "little bird". It had something to do with the way she opened her little mouth looking for food. So in rereading the account of Noah and the ark, it occurred to me for the first time that it wasn't a dove that Noah first sent out to look for dry land, it was a raven. "Raven" What a beautiful name for my dark skinned "little bird" that was born under a rainbow!

After we returned from Haiti, we got right to work updating our home study. I called our adoption agency and we forged into more paperwork. We began collecting the necessary paperwork, making appointments for fingerprinting, physicals, psychological evaluations and authentications of all of our documents. We also had to arrange a translator to translate our English documents into French, the official language of Haiti. There were a lot of hoops to jump through. Literally, blood, sweat and tears were involved in the process.

Considering how we were going to pay for this adoption

wasn't as terrifying as it had been for us the first time. I felt such

peace about it. I started to understand from our previous adoption

experience that if it were God's will, it was going to have to be His

bill. Having been home from Haiti just a few days, Todd got a

phone call one evening from a relative. "I have this Town and

Country Chrysler minivan that I would like to give to you. I just got

a new vehicle and I want you to have my used van." We then sold

our van for the exact cost of the twin's adoptions. Without

fundraising, striving, fretting, or trying to manifest the funds in our

own power, God supplied the need with one very unexpected phone

call.

"Is anything too hard for the Lord?"

Genesis 18:14

Because of some of the less than favorable responses to our

first adoption, we decided not to immediately share our wonderful

news with everyone. We decided to be a little more cautious about

who we told about our new adoption journey this time around.

While having lunch with a friend and her mother one afternoon, I was telling them about my concerns about the response we might get

when my friend's mom reminded me that we do not have to cast our

pearls before swine. I knew Jesus was actually referring to the

gospel in that teaching, but the meaning in that message still rang

true to me regarding our specific situation as I recalled some of the

opposition we faced during Adelyn's adoption.

The waiting for approval to travel to finalize the twins'

adoptions turned into nine long months. One day I was driving

down a five lane highway when I had a strange, overwhelming

feeling come over me. It felt like a supernatural kind of

unexplainable experience. It was like an abundant mixture of inner

peace, joy and contentment all at once. Then, there it was. Against

a very dark, gray, stormy afternoon sky was the biggest, most vivid

rainbow I had ever seen in my entire life right in front of me! I cried

tears of gratitude as I just had a knowing in my heart. It had finished

as it had begun, with that sign as a promise. When I got home, I

immediately called Gladys at the RAINBOW of Love Orphanage in

Port-Au-Prince to confirm in my mind what God had already

confirmed in my heart. Since she wasn't in, I left a voice message.

Later that day she returned my call and let me know that she was planning to call me to let me know that our adoptions had been approved and we could now make travel arrangements to return to Haiti to finalize the adoptions! God was faithful to keep His promise! Our rainbow twins were coming home!

Returning to Haiti the second time that year felt surreal. Upon picking my sister and me up from the airport, our appointed Haitian driver, Stanley, had been instructed to take us directly to the guesthouse. I would be taken to go to see the babies the following day was the plan. It was getting late in the evening and I knew full well that traveling in the dark was dangerous, but my mother's heart was only concerned with reconnecting with my precious little twins that I had left behind many months before. My obstinance paid off and I was able to convince our driver to take me to pick up the babies at the orphanage before heading to the guest house. My sister and I stood outside the white painted metal entrance gates in the pitch dark while the nannies quickly dressed the twins in the outfits I had sent for their homecoming and prepared them to meet us.

I cried tears of joy as I held both of my babies. Noah leaned away from me and looked as if he were extremely confused by this strange blanc (white) woman in front of him. Raven rested her sweet head trustingly on my shoulder as if she had been waiting for

me to come for her.

Haiti - October 6, 1999 Our driver Stanley, and Noreen
reconnecting with twins, Noah and Raven, after nine long months

We had been told Raven had been hospitalized. We had been

asked to pray in a letter update we had received a couple months

prior, but I didn't know how close we had come to losing her until

Gladys explained how serious Raven's condition had been.

Thankfully the Lord intervened and healed our baby girl without us

even knowing the severity of it all. Both Noah and Raven had some

sort of yeast infection that seemed to be due to excessive moisture in

the folds of their skin. It seemed to be in every crack and fold of

skin, under their armpits, in their necks and on their bottoms where it

was bad enough that there was some bleeding involved. We were able to get some cream from the pharmacy to treat their rashes and

we used some powder with cornstarch to help keep those moist areas

dry. It was becoming obvious that Doris' concerns about the quality

of care at that orphanage were accurate. The children were well fed,

dressed, and clean, but it seemed that they lacked nurturing,

affection and stimulation.

After we settled in back at home, Raven was sullen and

exceptionally quiet. Noah was not interested in human contact and

he cried a lot. He was emotionally distant and didn't reciprocate any

kind of affection. Neither of them seemed interested in playing with

toys. What little bit of training we had gotten through our adoption

agency was not enough to prepare us for the trials ahead. We did

our best to engage them, cuddle them and encourage age appropriate

play, but at the time I knew nothing about attachment disorder or its

effects on an infant's developing brain. In hindsight, I truly wish I

would have known then what I know now.

"Deprivation and harm suffered early in life

impact all the ways that a child develops –

coordination, ability to learn, social skills, size and

even the neurochemical pathways in the brain.

*These consequences can linger years *

after a child has left a life of hardship."

(The Connected Child, pg 2, Karyn B. Purvis David R. Cross Ph.D,

and Wendy Lyons Sunshine)

Noah and Raven had changed hands five times in their first ten months of life. They had lost their birthmother, then their foster mother (me), then the girls at Ebenezer Glenn Orphanage and then the nannies at Rainbow of Love Orphanage before they came home to live with us. That is a lot of disruption for a baby to experience, not to mention life in an institution can come with emotional and neurological consequences. Surely the nannies did their best to care for our children but it is not the same as living in a close family unit with attentive affection and continuous care of loving parents. We are very thankful for the life supporting care our children did receive while waiting to be adopted.

Raven and Noah - First Christmas 1999 - 11 months old

Chapter 5

Two By Two

"Enlarge your house; build an addition.

Spread out your home, and spare no expense!

For soon you will be bursting at the seams."

Isaiah 54: 2-3

The following summer, I had received a package in the mail that required a signature. On that day, our regular mail "man" had a substitute mail "lady". She seemed very friendly and excited about our dark skinned little ones running around the yard in the late summer sun. She openly shared that she and her husband had just begun researching adoption and she started asking a lot of questions. After speaking with her several times over the phone, I offered to help mentor them through their adoption and help them locate an eligible orphan that needed a family. Soon after Addie's adoption, I

had been asked by our agency if I would mentor a single mom

through the Haitian adoption process since they were only familiar

with Central America requirements, so I felt confident enough in

understanding the process that I could walk another family through

it.

Through some missionary friends, I contacted another

Haitian orphanage that was doing adoptions to see if they would be

willing to work with this new family seeking to adopt. To my

surprise, the directors of Haiti Children's Home, Pat Smith and her

daughter, Melinda Smith were staying with relatives just two hours

south of us in Jackson, Michigan. We loaded up some boxes with

new baby supplies for the orphanage and went to personally meet the

orphanage directors and inquire about the possibility of adopting

from Haiti Children's Home. My substitute mail lady was quite

excited about the possibilities as they showed us several pictures of

the children in need of families in their care. One picture stood out to

me in an unforgettable way. Her name was Sherlina (pronounced

Sha -leena). Melinda began to tell us her story and I couldn't help

but wonder, "Who is going to love her?" Her appearance was sadly disturbing, to say the least. Apparently a neighbor man had come to Pat and Melinda pleading with them to go rescue this little girl that would soon die of starvation if there were not some immediate intervention. Pat explained that they would have no legal right to take the child from her mother, so they asked him to encourage the mother to bring the child to them at the orphanage for help. The following day, the man brought the mother and her young daughter to the orphanage. The two year old's shallow breathing was a familiar sign that she probably would not survive the night. Melinda, who was a registered nurse, decided not to place a feeding tube down her because she believed that her condition had been allowed to decline past a point of no return and that it was too late for any intervention based on her experienced assessment. Melinda prayed over this tiny little soul and took her to bed with her because she didn't want her to take her final breaths and die alone in the night. That seemed to be the reality of this little one's desperate condition. Melinda explained to us how she had had the experience many times of helplessly watching babies and children die in her arms even after every desperate attempt, having been brought in for help too late. It sounded to her as if Sherlina was breathing her last breaths. It seemed obvious to her that this tiny one was close to

death. Miraculously, morning came and Sherlina was still alive!

With some new found hope, Melinda started an IV to give her some

extra fluids and placed a nasogastric feeding tube in her. They

bathed her and dressed her and watched as life slowly returned to her

frail, small ten pound frame.

  For several nights I woke up in the night and couldn't get

Sherlina's picture out of my mind. It wasn't a nightmare; it was

more horrific because it was real. I do not have access to that

original picture that may forever be ingrained in my memory. The

outline of her skull, her sunken cheeks and skin covered protruding

bones was something I'd only seen in National Geographic

magazines.

Sherlina

I shared Sherlina's story with Todd and after a few days of praying, together we decided that "we" would love her. I called Pat and Melinda as soon as we acknowledged and prayed for God's will for little Sherlina to join our family. Through the phone, I could hear Pat, Melinda's mother all the way from Haiti, shouting and praising God. She was so happy for Sherlina!

While initiating a home study update with our adoption agency, we started compiling a new list of possible little girl names and prayed for one suitable for Sherlina. Her new lease on life seemed deserving of a new name. We agreed on Livia Faith as our choice for our strong little survivor.

Shelina's mother relinquished her for adoption due to her inability to provide for her. Her father had abandoned them when she was an infant.

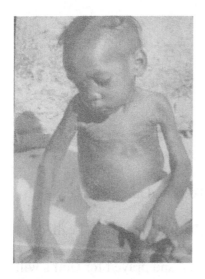

Sherlina 2 years old- several weeks into her recovery from severe malnutrition.

This photo came with a note that said; "Sherlina came to Haiti Children's Home near death. These pictures were taken several weeks after." I was also told that the little girl in the picture with Sherlina was the same age as her.

After the twins came home, we had surrendered and sold our

beautiful four bedroom, two bathroom, log dream home and built a

more practical six bedroom, three bathroom ranch home on a full

walkout basement giving us much more square footage for our

growing family.

Two months into updating our home study for Livia's

adoption, I read an article in a Christian magazine that challenged

me to broaden my perspectives. The overall message in the article

inspired me to question, "Would you build a canoe if God told you

to build an ark? Think bigger". I felt God was speaking and

challenging us again. We started to consider that the Lord might be

inspiring us to adopt one more in addition to Livia. Pat shared her

thoughts about a little girl about 18 months old she thought would be

a suitable match for us. We did not commit to taking sweet little

Hannah, but sort of explored all possibilities. We had never actually "looked" for or "chose" a specific child. God always seemed to orchestrate our circumstances and He had put all our adopted children in our path and on our hearts, thus far. It seemed that HE was doing the choosing about which children He had for us. Then we started to feel that maybe little Noah needed a little brother instead of another sister - he was already outnumbered three to one. So we looked into the baby boy possibilities. Once again, how do you choose one out of the many?

A good friend of mine was studying to become a social worker and had befriended Pat and Melinda from Haiti Children's Home. She started taking a big interest in their work there. She kept in closer contact than I had been even though our soon-to-be daughter Livia was still in their care. One day, just before she was leaving my house after a visit, she casually mentioned, "Did you know that Pat and Melinda took in a newborn three pound preemie baby boy?" I'm not sure if there are even words that can adequately explain this, but somewhere within a mother bear sort of feeling welled up inside of me. I was feeling extremely anxious and I wanted my friend to leave FAST so that I could go get in touch with Pat and question her about this new baby that had just arrived at the orphanage. "That was MY baby boy!" I knew it in my heart as if it were already a fact. I felt an instant attachment as soon as I heard he existed. I literally ran to my computer to shoot Pat an email and contact her about this new arrival at HCH. Sure enough, upon her quick reply, there was a new baby boy but she let me know that they had already assigned him to a waiting family in Canada. For the life of me, I could not understand it. How could this be?

In one of our previous adoption reference letters from a lifelong friend, I was described as being "Tenacious - determined; not willing to give up." In my heart, I knew that I knew that I knew that that baby was my son. I can't even begin to explain with words how that feels. It was a "knowing" that came from beyond my human comprehension. So I prayed. I didn't quit believing despite what the current circumstances seemed to dictate.

"Faith is not believing that God can, it is knowing that He will."

(Author unknown)

Approximately a week later, I got an unexpected email message from Pat in Haiti. She wanted to let me know that the couple from Canada that wanted to adopt Ducange decided to adopt a toddler age child rather than a newborn baby, so if we were still interested, he was all ours! Through many tears of gratitude, I thanked God for divinely and directly speaking to my heart and blessing us with another son! Pat was more than excited that prior to Ducange's birth, they had been gifted their first incubator from an organization in Canada. A very timely blessing for our three pound baby boy! We decided to name our new son, Ian Micah. Ian being a Hebrew form of the name John meaning "God is Gracious". He had been born on March 11, 2001.

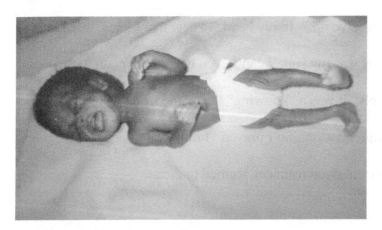

Three pound baby Ducange; aka Ian Micah

My mail lady friend and her husband had chosen to adopt a baby boy that had been abandoned at the orphanage as a newborn. A few months later, we traveled together to Haiti with a team of volunteers we had organized to work on some projects at the orphanage while we finalized our adoptions in order to bring our newest blessings home. We flew from Detroit, Michigan to Port-Au-Prince, Haiti and then made the three hour trip through the dark and pouring rain up "goat mountain" to the village of Mireabalais on the Eastern, Dominican side of Haiti. I knew we had a great team with us, as I heard from the cab of the truck song after song of loud praise and worship singing, intermingled with laughter above the sound of the thunder coming from the back of the beat up old Nisson pickup truck. As lightning flashed, I could see how close we were to the edge of the winding mountain road. Past the edge of the steep cliffs, I could also see remnants of rusted out old buses and vehicles that had obviously rolled over the cliff to their demise. The road was thick with mud and I prayed that we would not be the next vehicle to go over the edge of that mountain road. I had been warned that it was dangerous to drive at night and that that specific route was notorious for bandits stopping vehicles and people being robbed at gunpoint. (The pouring rain could have easily been God's protective hand at work.) Everyone was soaked to the skin, but we praised the Lord for our safe arrival at the orphanage late that night. We were able to meet and hold our dear little Ian, but Livia was asleep in a

crib they had set up for her in our room, so we just gazed at her as

she slept, trying not to disturb her.

Over the next few days, Livia attached to Todd much quicker

than she did to me. Pat shared that her mother had come to visit

several times but that Livia did not want anything to do with her.

Pat felt that in addition to being starved nearly to death, there

possibly was some other abuse going on there in that home. Livia's

mother came to meet us one day. We embraced and we both cried.

Melinda was surprised with this woman's change of heart; she had

always seemed so cold, untrusting, and her aunt had already

attempted to get her to change her mind about relinquishing Livia for

adoption. She was suspicious of American's motives for adopting

and did not support Livia's mother in the decision. When Melinda

came to join us on the front porch, she was so impressed she went to

get Pat - "You've GOT to see this!" The love of Christ broke

through our language barrier and Livia's two mothers instantly

experienced a deep mutual respect for one another. Livia quickly

decided I was the lesser of the two evils at that point and clung to me

while her mother was visiting. Ian's father also came with an aunt and a cousin to meet us. He was a quiet, reserved, tall man that truly cared about his infant son. Having lost his wife during the birth of Ian, and having no way to provide formula for the baby and having no way to take care of him, he sadly had no choice but to surrender him for adoption.

While we were staying at the orphanage, another adoptive mom flew in from Canada to finalize the adoption of her new Haitian daughter. She was a delight and we truly enjoyed getting to know her. She was a good and loving mother I could tell. She was very tender toward the little girl that now appeared very happy to have a mommy of her own. There had been many more Canadians adopting from this orphanage than Americans, so it didn't occur to me until late in our stay that this was the woman that originally was going to adopt our baby Ian! And that sweet little girl in her arms was the one that Pat had originally matched with us! We had traded babies and ended up in Haiti at the exact same time! We both praised the Lord; it was surely a divine appointment! What were the odds that we would ever actually meet and that God would steer us both to adopt the child that the other mom was originally matched with?

When we went to the American Embassy for our children's visa approval interview appointment, it was discovered that Ian's passport had the wrong birthdate on it so his visa to travel to the U.S. was denied. My heart was broken having strongly bonded and attached to my new four month old son. Pat did her best to console me as I totally experienced an emotional meltdown, not knowing what the future would hold and when or "if" I would ever see him again once I left Haiti. Todd and the team decided to take their scheduled flights home while I stayed on with Livia and Ian hoping for a rapid passport fix. Three weeks later, it became apparent that this could take more time than I had hoped. I was going to have to go back home to join my family and leave my baby Ian at the orphanage. I sobbed uncontrollably at the thought of walking away after we had bonded so quickly. I couldn't imagine my baby having had one on one tender care, going back to being one among the many motherless infants at the orphanage. Pat tried to console me, she encouraged me to think of Livia and her need for some individual attention. Our only option for return tickets at that time were first class seats with a flight departure date scheduled for August 8th, 2001, Livia's third birthday. Ironically, Livia's departure from her destitute beginnings, having lived in extreme poverty, was a stark contrast to her "first class" departure from Haiti. Her life was about to change dramatically.

Even though I realized that it was good for Livia to be the only baby for a while, my heart still ached for my sweet little Ian. After a thorough physical including a series of blood tests it was determined that Livia had high levels of lead poisoning in her blood. We were told that through a normal high protein diet with good nutrition, her levels would come down, which thankfully, they did. In questioning Pat and Melinda about this, they explained that when there isn't enough food, the Haitian mothers often make cakes of mud from the ground and feed them to their children to fill their hollow, empty stomachs. The lead is in the mud.

Livia was a happy little girl who adapted well to her new family and new environment. Her twin siblings were much taller than her even though they were five months younger. She was quite short and small for her age although she had filled out quite a bit over the past several months. I had asked nurse Melinda from Haiti Children's Home what I should tell the pediatrician once I got her in for a physical exam. Melinda said, "You tell him her life has just begun." Livia was settling in nicely by the time Ian was finally

cleared to come home in late December just before Christmas.

Livia Faith Weaver, 3 years old

        A missionary friend of mine offered to escort Ian to the states

once his passport issue had been fixed and his new corrected

passport had been issued. Just prior to Christmas, my mail lady

friend offered to drive me to Miami, Florida so I could reunite with

our now nine month old son. As soon as I reached out for Ian at the

airport, he eagerly leaned into my arms, held onto my hair with his

right hand, sucked his left thumb and laid his head on my shoulder.

After our long four month separation, he almost seemed to be feeling

the same level of contentment and relief that I was feeling at that

moment.

Noreen and Ian, Miami International Airport, December 2001

Stopping at a southern Michigan McDonalds on our route to Florida, my friend had called her husband and explained the strange sound our vehicle was making. We didn't know if we should continue on or turn back for home but decided to continue on. After returning from Florida, my friend's husband, who was a mechanic by trade, discovered that we had driven approximately 2,988 miles on a cracked, broken flywheel. He did me the favor of explaining the mechanical problem, the function of a flywheel and explained how "miraculous" it was that the flywheel stayed in place for the duration of our trip. I praised God for His watchful care over us.

Ian Micah Weaver, 1 year old

Chapter 6

African Blessings

"You can make many plans, but the Lord's purpose will prevail."

Proverbs 19:21

As a little girl, I dreamed of having twelve children and going to visit Africa one day. Those dreams faded over the years and became what seemed like less and less of a possibility. For nine years, Todd and I were quite content with our sweet family of six, having two beautiful daughters and two wonderful sons. The perfect sized family, I thought. Then after our five Haitian adoptions, my dear friend, Anita King from Maryland, who had a similar passion for orphans, started facilitating Liberian adoptions for West African Children's Support Network (WACSN). She told me about a little two year old girl that was relinquished for adoption. Her name was

Esther Williams and that was all the information that was available. The civil war had ravaged the country. Many men were forced to fight or flee. It was thought that this little girl's daddy fled to neighboring Sierra Leone. Due to his desperate situation, it was believed that possibly he abandoned his family so that he could spare his own life. Esther's mother, being destitute and alone, took her toddler to an orphanage funded by WACSN and relinquished her for adoption believing that to be the best option for her daughter.

I knew that if we were to adopt her, we would need to change her name and find one more suitable and pleasing to my ear! "Esther" sounded so old fashioned, but every time I wanted to consider looking into other names, for some reason, I just couldn't! We had a name and an approximate age but no photo and no other specific information about her, yet the Lord so strongly laid it upon our hearts to adopt her that we went ahead by faith and committed to starting the paperwork for her adoption having not even yet seen her face. Prior to seeing her picture for the first time, the Lord spoke to me in a powerful way. I was convinced that He did not want us to change her name. It helped that my mother, our #1 adoption supporter and encourager at the time absolutely LOVED the name! I decided I would learn to like it and live with it if it were God's will. In the near future, I would find out the reason why I felt so strongly about keeping her name even though it wasn't a name I would have chosen.

After completing five Haitian adoptions, it seemed Liberian adoptions were extremely quick and efficient! The country's requirements were minimal and the official language of Liberia was English, so none of our documents nor the authentications for those numerous documents had to be translated!

In a few short months Esther's adoption was final and a Liberian escort from West African Children's Support Network volunteered to meet me in Washington, D.C. on Thanksgiving Day 2004. It almost felt like living a dream as I embraced my teeny little African princess. I immensely enjoyed my one night alone with Esther in the hotel in Washington, D.C. before we flew back to Michigan the following day to our house full of bigger blessings. Esther was definitely small for her age and was suffering from intestinal parasites (giardia) which she managed to eventually share with her daddy before she was able to overcome it with medication.

She acclimated quickly to her new and different surroundings and

seemed to enjoy being the baby of the family.

Esther and her biological mother, Musu

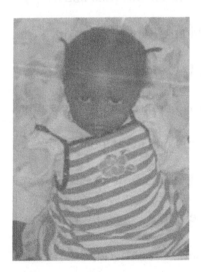

Our first pictures of Esther in dresses we had sent for her to Liberia

November 2004, Ronald Reagan Washington National Airport –

Esther and Noreen

A couple months later, at the beginning of the following year,

I started working with my two precious friends, Anita King who

lived in Maryland and Pam Gremillion who lived in Tennessee, on

facilitating Liberian adoptions for West African Children's Support

Network. It was a desire of my heart to find Christian homes for

orphaned children who needed the love, structure and blessing of a

family.

One day Sister Pam sent me a photo listing of available

children waiting to be adopted. I saw a grainy computerized picture of a little eight year old girl among the many listed and I

immediately sensed that there was something VERY special about

that dear one! There wasn't much info about her, only that her

mother wanted her to be adopted so that she did not become "a child

mother." I quickly learned that in Liberia, prostitution is how girls

and women survive. I shared my thoughts with Pam about this girl

named Grace and she agreed with my interpretation of this special

little girl. She explained that she and her husband had had the same

feeling and that they were praying about adopting her. My heart

sank as I was sure God was speaking to me about her as well.

Grace – 8 years old, Liberia

A few days went by and I got a rare phone call from Sister Pam. Our communications had mainly been through emails. When I picked up the phone, I heard her high-pitched, chipper, unforgettable voice, "Sister Nor-een?" (I absolutely adored her sweet southern drawl!) "Brother Charles and I have been praying on our knees about adopting Grace and God made it known to us that she is not to be our daughter. We found out that Grace has a sibling in the United States and we strongly believe that God wants her to be placed with her sister. Our conversation ended on that note. It seemed that neither one of us would be adopting this very "special" little girl.

Within another week or maybe two, I got another surprising phone call from a VERY excited Sister Pam. "Sister Nor-een! You had better sit down." I laughed, wondering what could be so serious between us that I needed to sit down. "Sister Nor-een! I just found out that Grace is your daughter Esther's half-sister! God wants Grace to be YOUR daughter!!" I was once again in awe, knowing that these circumstances were definitely inspired by the Lord. Todd was at his weekly Friday morning Bible Study breakfast at his friend Ralph's house. I called there immediately to talk to him and tell him about my conversation with Pam. In my imagination, I expected that Todd was not going to be accepting of another addition to our family, let alone an eight year old who could come with all kinds of serious emotional baggage. I proceeded carefully and explained every detail of the story I had just heard. I begged him, please don't say no, just ask the men to pray with you and ask God what His will is for us and for Grace in this situation.

I dreaded Todd's return because I was already pessimistically sure he was NOT going to be real supportive of this one. The adoption of Esther just months prior was somewhat of a stretch for him. I prayed a similar prayer like I had done when we were first adopting Adelyn; "Lord, I will not beg or argue with my husband to control this situation. If it is your will, Lord You must place it upon his heart to walk into this adoption." When Todd got home my heart raced. I had decided not to even mention Grace's adoption although it was all I could think about. As I was putting some things away in the kitchen, Todd came in and put his arms around me from behind. I turned around to see a huge grin on his face. Little did I know that God had already prepared a personal message for Todd that morning also. He explained to me how, before Ralph's wife had gone to work, she had written an acronym message on a chalkboard in their

kitchen over the table where they had held their Bible Study:

GOD'S

RICHES

AT

CHRIST'S

EXPENSE

The writing was literally on the wall. The men did pray with

Todd, but it seemed to all of them that God had already spoken and

there was not much considering or praying left to do. There was no

question about it; we were being blessed with yet another beautiful

daughter!

Sister Pam kept the photo listings coming. I had found three

Christian families that were willing to adopt six of the available

orphaned children. When an adorable five year old girl showed up

on my computer, I went the extra mile to reach out, trying to find

her a family and rescue her from the grip of poverty and the great

possibility that she too might be forced into prostitution in order to

survive. Sadly most people were more interested in adopting an infant or a toddler so five years of age seemed to be a stretch. I was frustrated that I wasn't getting any responses. Once again, "There is something about her….." I kept thinking. After many attempts to make a connection with a possible Christian family for her, I mentioned something to Sister Pam. She laughed at me. "Sister Noreen, do you think God might be telling you this little girl is YOUR daughter?" I found out that her name was Esther Williams. WHAT? Esther Williams was our daughter! We had already adopted an Esther Williams! Ironically, their mothers also shared the same first name of Musu. We effortlessly walked into this adoption as well, believing God was the author of every coincidence and circumstance. We had several discussions on how we might handle having two daughters with the same name. We decided we would consider the options and allow our new, older daughter Esther to help us decide.

Jenaya Esther- 5 years old, Liberia, West Africa

God blessed us with another uneventful adoption process much like our first Liberian adoption experience and in early July 2005 we got word that we could travel to West Africa to pick up our girls! Arriving in Liberia was quite an experience! The airport was quite primitive. Even Haiti's Port-au-Prince airport was bigger and more modern. After collecting our luggage and supplies we found our connections and piled in our waiting vehicle. Apparently there had been some miscommunication or something. I was a little confused when I was asked why I had come so soon, the paperwork wasn't ready yet and I was told that we might not have visa approval before our return scheduled flights. I expressed very little concern as

I let them know that we were not in control but that God was. There

was no mistake; we would simply trust God in the timing. Maria

Luyken, founder and director of WACSN (West African Children's

Support Network) then let me know that there had been some talk

about me prior to my arrival. "Sister Pam said that if it had to

happen to anyone, you were the one that could handle it."

Apparently not everyone can see the adventure in being stuck in a

country with no infrastructure for an indefinite period of time? I

laughed at the compliment.

The next day I met our girls for the first time. They seemed

extremely excited to see me and they giggled as I began to mother

them with hugs. We had packed little backpacks with gifts and

small treasures to keep them occupied at the guesthouse and on the

plane for their long journey home. Crayons, color books, notepads,

a new dolly for each, a dress, socks and a pair of brand new shiny

white shoes were enclosed in each gift bag. Esther was the first to

speak, "I have PLENTY!" she loudly and joyously exclaimed upon

examining her new personal possessions. Another family from the

eastern part of the states was also there to adopt three year old twin

girls. I thought it funny that our girls were so thrilled that they got the plump mother and the twins got the thin mother! In their culture, as in Haiti, being on the heavy side was a sure sign of wealth and/or prosperity. They believed, by looking at me, that they would never lack for food and to them that was a good sign! I had never experienced being heavy as a blessing until that day.

One day while hanging out at the guest house, Grace brought me a picture she had drawn in her new notebook. Feeling very proud of her accomplishment, I noticed that she seemed to be looking for approval on my face. I smiled at her then looked at the picture she had so carefully drawn in detail. My heart despaired when I realized that this little girl had witnessed some very violent acts while the civil war raged around her. She had drawn a picture of a man holding what looked like a machine gun while shooting another man that was facing him. Stories came tumbling out of graphic war scenes that surely would have caused the strongest adult to suffer from posttraumatic stress disorder. I feared what emotional scars this young girl would have. Her recent memories of running from rebel soldiers came forth with little emotion as if it were a common occurrence in everyone's life. This civil war for Liberia resulted in the deaths of many civilians and thousands of displaced people, and our two girls had obviously witnessed many casualties.

Having been forced to flee their home in the bush of Bong County,

Grace described their experience, "We were RUNNING and

RUNNING and RUNNING!" Some vague stories spilled forth of

burning cars and innumerable dead bodies they witnessed on their

dangerous journey to the capital city of Monrovia. In my mind I

envisioned images of gory scenes from the previous genocide in

Rwanda. I could not imagine what these girls had experienced. I

recalled the warnings from our adoption agency's director, "At eight

years old, this little girl is going to come with some baggage."

Grace and her biological mother, Musu

While in Liberia, I had the privilege of meeting Grace and

our youngest Esther's birth mother. I was very curious and very thankful for the opportunity to ask her why she gave Esther her name. I did not understand its significance although I just somehow felt that it definitely had one. Although English was the official language of Liberia, understanding the Liberian's words and speech was quite difficult. With the help of an interpreter, Musu slowly recounted the story for me.

> July of 2002 was a very difficult time in Liberia. The war was devastating. Being full of despair, Musu named her new newborn infant a Bassa tribal name Ju-Say-Doh that was synonymous for "destitute", I was told. Her uncle, a Liberian Pastor, told Musu that this was no name for a child and that he would pray and ask God to show him what the baby's name should be. One night, Musu's uncle had a dream. He saw a white sheet as if hanging down from the sky. In big bold letters he saw a name written in black against the white background.
>
> E S T H E R
>
> Musu's uncle told her that the Lord had given him the name ESTHER. That would be the name of her newborn daughter. I could hardly believe my ears. No wonder God would not allow us to change her name! According to

Musu's Uncle, God was the one who chose her name. And

it had a profound, special significance to her biological

family.

Esther Joy Weaver- 3 years old

During our stay in Liberia, we were very blessed to be

invited to visit a school that had just started in a remote village

outside of the capital of Monrovia. The children recited songs and

scriptures for us before lunch was provided for the children and then

we handed out gift packages with the usual treasures of

toothbrushes, toothpaste, soap, wash clothes, pencils, and a small

toy. There were close to eighty children in attendance. I was

blessed by their joyful participation and their sincerity when praying while sitting on old wooden benches. There was mud under their feet from the rain that couldn't be contained by the old thatched roofing and lack of exterior walls. I took up a large serving spoon and took my place at the huge cauldron of what looked like slop; a mixture of different foods containing corn mush, sliced hot dogs, oatmeal, beans, etc. The children had brought their own bowls, plates or whatever they could find to contain their precious gift of food. It saddened my heart to see some of their bowls, some of which looked much older and dirtier than the dishes our dogs ate from at home. After prayer, they quietly and obediently lined up and we began filling their bowls. I watched in horror as these sweet little children voraciously devoured the contents like starving animals without any utensil but their fingers. I had never seen hunger like this. Tears filled my eyes as it was announced that there was more to be served if anyone wanted seconds. I watched as an uncontrollable mob of children pushed and shoved, knocking over the younger children to get one more scoop of the coveted slop. The principal worked to regain some order but for a few minutes there was utter chaos. They obviously had not eaten recently and they probably didn't know when their next meal might come. Most of these children were orphans of war. My mind went back to the

moments prior recalling their joyful singing and clapping and

smiling … all the while, these children were seriously hungry!

Suddenly I was convicted of all the times I had complained about

minor irritations. I could not seem to grasp the entire experience, it

was all so overwhelming, but I did recognize that I was in the

presence of Jesus. I could sense His presence like never before in

my life. In my mind I questioned, "Is this where we find you,

Lord?" The Creator and Savior of the world is literally found among

"the least of these"? As Matthew 25:40 tells us, when we serve the

vulnerable, we are literally serving Him.

Orphans of war. Liberia, West Africa 2005

Although it initially seemed like an impossibility to Maria, the adoption paperwork quickly came together and we were able to finalize the adoptions and meet with the consulate to obtain their visas. We did have to delay our return flight back to the states, but we only had to extend our stay for a few extra days. Within that time, Maria was able to finalize the adoptions of three other children as well, so my friend Geri (who had traveled with me) and I traveled back home escorting five children. In addition to our eight year old Grace and five year old Esther, we had an eighteen month old baby boy and nine month old boy/ girl twins! It was a tremendous blessing to take part in helping these families unite with their little ones, but the twenty hour flight with layovers in Ghana and London were quite memorable with five children in tow, three of which were in diapers! We praised God for the short delay in our adoption paperwork so that we could accompany these precious children to their awaiting families.

Esther and Grace saying goodbye at the orphanage where they lived prior to their adoption

Once we arrived home, we had a lot of adjustments to make. A light switch, a bathtub, running water at the sink, a flushing toilet, and cupboards filled with things were all new experiences for our African blessings. At first, communication was difficult. Although English is the official language of Liberia, they had a strong accent and they used much different wording and spoke very fast, therefore their speech was difficult for us to understand. Our new Esther was willing and agreed to allow us to call her Jenaya Esther, which was the name we had chosen for her before I had left for Liberia.

Thankfully the girls embraced their new life with us.   Even at five

and eight years old, it seemed as if they never looked back. They

never experienced any nightmares or crying or sleepless nights nor

did they express any desire to return. We were so grateful to God

for how easily they acclimated to all things new.

Chapter 7

Jungle Adventures

"Faith is taking the first step

even when you can't see the whole staircase."

Author Unknown

"God teach us how to live in this world and not be part of it," had become a focused prayer of our hearts. "What is your will for us God?"

On January 8, 2008, we determined to literally leave all and follow after Christ on a whole new level. Todd left his stable job of 25 years as a custom welder and crew leader at a large manufacturing company. We walked away from all the securities of life; family, friends, the benefits of insurance, steady income, modern conveniences and life as we knew it, determined to trust God only and depend on Him for our every need. We set about the overwhelming task of deciding what to do with every material thing that we had accumulated over 28 years - sell it, trash it, give it away or take it with us? The sale of our home and some inherited property funded our relocation to Belize, Central America. At this time, we had twelve children, of which ten were still living at home. Our oldest son decided to make the leap of faith adventure with us to live in the jungle rainforest as independent missionaries. Our youngest biological son, who was eighteen at the time, decided to stay and move in with one of our older daughters who as an adult had already been living on her own. We filled out and applied for eleven

passport renewal applications and acquired the required

documentation from our vet for our dear dachshund friend, Oscar

and our two new German Shepherd pups, Zada and Zara to travel

with us as well. After a lot of serious fasting, prayer and research,

we felt quite comfortable with settling in the beautiful, tropical and

humid country of Belize. It was a relatively safe place for expats to

live and if necessary, the distance (through Mexico) from the USA

could be driven. After giving away and selling most of our

belongings, we filled a 12 foot UHaul truck and our 12 passenger

van with the necessities of life for eleven people and hired a

respected relocation management company that our realtor had

suggested to drive our things through Mexico.

I soon realized that one very difficult, yet good thing about

the jungle is the lack of worldly distractions! No radio, no

television, no newspapers, no internet, and a phone that rarely ever

worked! I quickly discovered that when you remove all the

distractions, and it's just you and God, you begin to see yourself a

little more as He does. For me, that was not exactly a pretty picture.

Our goal was to become independent sheep farmers, relying on and depending on the Lord to provide all our needs. I believe our kind

heavenly Father taught us valuable lessons we could not have

learned any other way had we not journeyed to the jungle. It was

definitely bigger than a leap of faith; actually it felt more like

intentionally walking off the edge of a cliff and expecting God to

catch us.

While we searched for property to build or buy a home, we

rented a home in San Ignacio in the Northwest part of the country

that bordered Guatemala. Todd and I had made a preliminary trip

alone several months prior to search out real estate, so we had some

idea of what was available.

After visiting most parts of the small country, we took up

residence in the small mountainous village of Santa Marta about

thirty miles south of the capital city of Belmopan. In spite of some

warnings about the dangers of living among some of these village

residents that apparently practiced witchcraft, we found a secluded

twenty acre piece of property on the furthest interior edge of the

village. It was a cement block home that was finished and fully

furnished on the upper level, built by an American couple originally

from New Mexico. To prevent the possibility of flood water

damage, it had been built on cement pillars twelve feet in the air.

After purchasing the property, our neighbors proudly shared with us

that our village was known as "The Treasure of Belize".

Interestingly, we were surrounded by hills and mountains that

protected us from the worst insults of hurricanes and flash flooding.

Our village was named after St. Margaret of Scotland, a Scottish

Saint well known for her kindness to the poor and orphans which

ironically and accurately described our passion and purpose in living

there.   The official language was English although most Belizeans

were immigrants from neighboring Central American countries who

spoke only Spanish. Thankfully the children were taught to speak

English in school, so our best translators were always the children.

It was there in that humid, tropical jungle environment that

my senses awakened to many new things. For the first time, I was

able to hear a mother hen lovingly "talk" to her newly hatched baby

chicks as she showed them where to find treasures of insects and

edible delights hidden in the grass. I heard the sound of a ewe

speaking comfort to her newborn lamb and I heard the sweet sounds

of a cow gently calling to her new baby calf. Daily I awakened to

the 4 AM sounds of deep throated howler monkeys communicating with one another. Multitudes of nocturnal croaking frogs and

singing insects came to life as the jungle grew dark each night. I

saw iguanas climbing trees, armadillos crossing the road, monstrous

tarantulas walking gracefully across our lawn and giant snakes

slithering effortlessly through our garden. I tasted the yummy, juicy

sweetness of fresh pineapple, limes, grapefruits, guava, apple

bananas, plantains, breadfruit and avocados picked straight from

trees and plants growing in our own backyard. I gained a whole new

respect for the gift of creation as I witnessed and heard things I'd

never heard before or taken the time to appreciate.

Among our personal belongings, we also had shipped many

boxes of items to donate to the poor among us. These items had sat

in plastic totes for several months as we pondered what to do with it

all. A Pastor of a church in our village was actually our closest

neighbor and his family became our closest friends although he and

his wife spoke only Spanish. One evening they came to visit with

their five children as interpreters. An idea came to my mind and I

asked if they would be the vessels to hand out our gifts of food,

clothing, shoes, and additional items through their church. They

were very thankful for the opportunity and talked about gathering some volunteers to help organize the project. As we went to look

into the large plastic totes and cardboard boxes, my dear Belizean

neighbor, sister, and friend Maria declared in Spanish, "This is from

the Lord!" The first box she opened was filled with baby clothing,

diapers, rubber pants, receiving blankets, bottles and toys. Little did

we know that a baby girl had just been born in our village in a hut

across the road from our property just the night before. Maria went

on to say that the mother had NOTHING for this baby. She

explained that the father was an alcoholic and was rarely at home

and was not responsible or interested in taking care of the needs of

his family. We all praised the Lord together for the way He supplied

a need while supplying us with an avenue and an opportunity to

share the love of Christ with our neighbors.

Noreen & Neighbor with her baby

It was in Belize that I learned (out of necessity) how to minimize and become more frugal.   I became a great fan of Carla Emery's "Country Living Encyclopedia".   Through her instruction, I learned how to dry can beans, make homemade sour cream, how to make a variety of cheeses, homemade crackers, sourdough bread, planting according to the moon and the seasons, harvesting, butchering, how to raise goats, and other very practical advice. After our washing machine died, we resorted to washing all our laundry by hand. Mostly we used buckets and tubs, but during the dry season we were forced to go to the river for bathing and laundering since our water well and our creek always ran completely dry. We usually used bars of Fels Naptha laundry soap and scrubbed everything by hand, hanging clothes on the line in the yard during the dry season and hanging them under the house in the rainy season. To save on propane gas we often enjoyed cooking our meals over an open fire pit outside.

Nights were extremely dark and noisy in the jungle. One night there seemed to be some additional commotion going on outside that caused Todd enough concern that he decided to go outside to check to see what was going on. I prayed specifically for safety and reminded God of how we trusted in Him as our protector. I fought against fear as I prayed. Before long Todd came back to our room to announce that he hadn't found anything out of order. As we climbed back into bed, I felt a terrible, painful stinging sensation on my right big toe. I knew immediately that I had been stung by a scorpion. I jumped up and ran to the bathroom and sat on the toilet and told Todd I could not go back to bed until that arachnid was found and killed! I knew from previous warnings about any sting or bite or any poisonous encounter that staying calm was important. An increased heart rate would only cause the poison to circulate through the bloodstream more rapidly. It helped to know that the scorpion stings in Belize are not deadly, just painful. Todd looked on the bed and in the blankets and on the floor for the scorpion that had stung me. As he searched the dark room with a flashlight, he heard and felt a crunch under one foot. Sure enough, he accidently stepped on our unwelcome visitor and we were finally able to settle down and get some sleep.

Once we ventured to look at some sheep in a well-known area of Belize called Spanish Lookout. The only way to access it was to take an old rickety ferry across the river.

This was a Mennonite settlement that had modern, American type stores where we could pretty much shop for anything we needed. After making arrangements to meet up with the rancher that owned the sheep, we found the place where he lived a few miles out of town. Unknown to us, he kept his sheep at a different location closer to the Guatemalan border. My eyes must have been bulging from my head as four men with what appeared to be big assault rifles climbed into the back of our trailer with no explanation. We had to drive another ten miles to a very remote area to go to where they said they kept the sheep. Without offering to come along, the rancher told us these men would take us to where he kept his sheep. I sincerely believed that there was a strong possibility that this was the end of us. I had formulated in my mind that these men were

certainly going to rob and kill us "Americans" and steal our van and

trailer. Other than by the word of a stranger, we had no reason to

trust them or believe they were actually taking us to find sheep. The

road became narrower and narrower with jungle overgrowth on both

sides and I felt a dark sense of doom. Todd was concerned, I could

tell, but not as concerned as I was, or maybe he was just hiding it

better. Would we be kidnapped? I prayed, "Oh Lord please be with

us, please protect us. But Lord, if we are coming home today, I pray

we are ALL ready to meet you face to face." We had all gone along

for this trip so there were eleven of us in the van, and everyone

seemed quieter than normal and a bit nervous. Soon we came to a

place with a gate and one of the men jumped out of the trailer to

unlock it so we could continue on as we drove up a steep hill. To

my amazement, we saw a small caretaker's house, and a corral with

sheep in the near distance! I was still feeling unsure and

traumatized, but thankful we at least had reached some sheep!

Instead of telling us prior to the trip, we were informed at that time

that the men with the guns were actually along for our protection!

Being so close to the Guatemalan Border there were risks of being robbed and killed along the way! I had no idea the ones I feared that

might take my life were actually there to protect it! Thankfully we

were blessed to be able to invest in two rams to add to our herd that

day before we safely traveled the one hour trip back to our village

without incident. What a relief! We all praised God for His

watchful care over us and laughed at how wrong we had been about

the protection of the armed men riding in the back of our trailer.

As a member of our family, Oscar, our oldest son's seven

year old dachshund, was one of those dogs who truly thought he was

one of us. His mental capacity reminded me of an adolescent child.

He knew what he liked and what he did not like and he wasn't afraid

to let us know. He was definitely a dog with an attitude and a unique

personality. He refused pancakes without syrup, and would only eat

the most buttery morsels of popcorn. He loved Doritos but only the

original flavor chips and only the ones with an extra thickness of

cheesy seasoning.

Oscar seemed to enjoy Belizean afternoon naps in our

screened in porch, and hunting for toads and frogs that congregated

in the green foliage around the house. He enjoyed being with and

working alongside Todd and the children as they cleared a fence line for our soon to be new milk cow, Bertha. One early morning after

breakfast, Todd and the children all went out to clear overgrowth and

brush for the new cow pen. Within a short time, they brought Oscar

up to the house and told me he had been bitten by a snake. He was

dripping blood from a bite to his nose, but as I held him, he seemed

to act as if it didn't bother him. At the time we didn't know if we

should be concerned or not.   Little did I know then that his blood

that was contaminated by the hemotoxin from a venomous snake

could have entered my bloodstream as well through the numerous

fresh open bug bites I had all over my ankles and bare feet. Todd

made sure all of the children were safely up near the house, then he

took his machete in hand and walked back to where Osar had the

snake encounter. He hacked away at the thick brush until he saw the

coiled snake ready to strike again! As adrenaline rushed, Todd

chopped and chopped away at the snake determined that it would not

have the opportunity to bite anyone or anything else. He learned

after the fact that God definitely protected him. He apparently had

not handled that situation with the pit viper well. We learned later

on that these particular snakes can still bite and inject venom even

with a head severed from its body. Our neighbor friend was an adventure tour guide for a popular tourist attraction in a neighboring

village. He identified the snake as a Yellow Jaw, aka Tommy Goff,

aka Fer-de-Lance. We also learned that these particular poisonous

and deadly snakes are extremely aggressive and territorial. They are

one of Belize's eight venomous snakes, and some say they are the

most dangerous.

Oscar

Our son stayed with Oscar as he passed away in the night.

Due to the hemotoxin in the snake's venom, his bleeding never

stopped. Oscar died a hero in my eyes. We were so grieved to lose

such a close friend yet so thankful for the sacrifice he made for our

family. It was a tragic loss, but we were beyond thankful that

providentially God allowed Oscar to discover that snake before it

had a chance to strike one of our children or anyone else.

Soon after Oscar's death, we also had a very close encounter with a very large eight foot long boa constrictor that the neighbor boys had brought over to proudly show us. They had killed it while hoeing weeds at their family farm just down the road from us. Their dad was not too happy about their trophy snake. He said boas were an asset to the farm by eating the rodents that were eating their produce.

Eight foot long Boa constrictor

Noah and the (dead) Boa constrictor

After losing Oscar, our son decided to purchase a dog that would be more of an asset to the farm. It seemed that Australian Cattle Dogs, aka Blue Heelers, were widely respected in Belize as a loyal and fierce defender of family, farm, animals and property. Most people were afraid of them, so we felt that maybe it might be good to have a dog like that around. News spread quickly throughout the village and even the neighbor boys jokingly told us they wouldn't be coming over to visit us anymore! Kody showed us quickly how smart and intuitive he was. He learned fast and was very willing to please. As an older pup, he took it upon himself to help us separate our milk cow from the bull in the pasture as we tried to lead her to the barn for milking. He would nip at the heels of the bull and quickly circle him to prevent getting kicked. His behavior was entirely instinctual; we never trained him to do that. We started calling upon Kody to help round up the sheep when they would get out of their pen. Pretty soon we didn't even have to go out to take care of the problem. We could just yell, "Kody, sheep"! And he would chase them back under the fence. Interestingly, after a while, the sheep would hear us say "Kody, sheep!" and they would run

back under the fence and put themselves away, anticipating his

nipping bites to their heels!

One day, Todd and the children were out under the shade of

the sheep shelter in the corral spreading sheets to hang so we could

dry our pinto bean crop. From the house, I could see and hear Kody

jumping up in the air and barking at something in the tall pasture

grass several feet from the corral. Upon investigating his find, we

discovered that he was entertaining a young yellow jaw, putting

himself between his family and the snake. That evening we

discovered Kody's nose was swelling. I felt a sick, sinking feeling

in my stomach as we realized he too had been bitten by a venomous

viper. We didn't expect him to make it, but we prayed for our

fearless friend and gave him an aspirin to reduce the swelling in desperation, not knowing what else to do. The next day, Kody slept a lot and was not himself. We hoped and prayed that he didn't get enough of the venom to kill him. For a second time, God used a dog to come between a deadly enemy and our family. Incidentally, our neighbor friend had also warned us that the young yellow jaws were even more deadly than the adults because they had not yet learned how to control the amount of venom they released at each bite.

On our property, we planted several lime trees, banana plants, over two hundred pineapple plants, and many papaya trees that I had started from the seeds of fruit we had purchased and eaten from the open market. We grew a wonderful garden of sweet potatoes, cassava, okra, corn and several different kinds of beans. Some days I felt so overwhelmingly blessed, as if we were living in our own mini garden of Eden!

On one occasion, my sister ZoAnn and my brother-in-law Rex came to visit us. They were frequent visitors on the island of Caye Caulker where they enjoyed annual extended vacations since their retirement. By this point, we were very much at the end of our resources. We had basics but not many extra groceries to work with for our own needs let alone much of anything extra to share with our company. Maybe out of pride, we didn't really share with anyone

just how poor we had become. Somehow we pulled together a taco

feast complete with homemade salsa, homemade sour cream and

homemade mozzarella cheese made from milk from our cow,

homemade refried beans, homemade tortillas and our home grown

chicken. From the limes given from a neighbor's orchard, we made

delicious lime bars for dessert. Our guests were quite thrilled and

impressed with our fresh, all natural home cooked meal. Later,

while relaxing and visiting that evening with my sister, she presented

me with a $1,000 check. "Here", she said, "We really appreciate

what you are doing here and we want to help out." I tried to

maintain my composure, but my heart must have skipped a beat as I

silently thanked the One who had inspired their extremely generous

gift.

We were blessed by the good advice from neighboring

farmers as to how to protect our sheep herd from the possibility of an

unwelcome jaguar or cougar attack. We put cow bells around a few

of the sheep's necks to scare away any big cats as some suggested.

Others told us to put solar lights along the corral and fence posts.

Some suggested keeping dogs in the yard, which we already had our two German Shepherds and our little Oscar roaming the place. A

forestry and wildlife team visited our farm once and questioned us

about any sightings or incidents of jaguar attacks. They

complimented us on how we had set up the corral near the house

where the smell of humans could also be a deterrent. According to

them, we seemed to be doing everything right! Even though we

anticipated possible problems with jaguars devouring our livestock,

as it turned out, intestinal parasites were actually the enemy we

should have been most concerned about. In spite of frequent and

consistent doses of Ivermectin, our sheep were slowly dying.

Todd dug far too many graves by hand as we consistently

experienced loss after loss. As our sheep began to die, one by one

our wooly investments were frequently buried in the rocky hard soil

of our 20 acre farm. Out of frustration, one day our son asked the twelve year old son of our neighboring Pastor friend what he thought could be causing the death of our livestock. The young boy quickly and confidently replied, "Satan wants you to repent for coming here." We were amazed at his answer. We were looking for a solution to this problem never expecting this boy would express that there may be a spiritual connection to our circumstances. One by one our mothers, their babies and our rams were dying, in spite of all our best efforts to treat them with a broad spectrum anti parasite medication. Our young twelve year old Belizean friend taught us an important lesson. EVERYTHING is spiritual.

Through all of this, the Lord showed us how our own worst deadly enemy is not an external force of any kind, but our greatest most dangerous enemy is the enemy within. The condition of our heart will surely define our eternity, not what anyone says, thinks, believes or does to us. Apart from Christ, spiritual death comes through the internal parasites of bitterness, resentments, unforgiveness, hatred, jealousy, anger, envy, greed, and sin of every kind. No vicious outside influence of any kind can determine our destiny. We are just like sheep, choosing if we will follow the Good

Shepherd and abide in the Lord Jesus Christ, the sinless Lamb of God, our only hope for eternal life and salvation.

As we prepared to sell our home and leave our rainforest abode, we met an American man that had been staying in our village. He was from Wisconsin and was working as a chauffeur for a non driving, horse and buggy conservative Christian family that was visiting in a very conservative community in Belize known as Springfield, not far from our village. They were planning to return to the states so we made plans to follow their driver through Mexico since he had had experience having done this before. We had not yet decided if we would be moving back to the states permanently or if we would return in the near future, but we did trust that God would show us His will for us. After almost two years living in Belize, the Lord provided us with a way to return to the states and make a fresh start. In spite of our very real struggle, we will be forever thankful for having had the experience and the hard lessons we learned there were invaluable.

Not too far into our journey in driving back to the states, the new tarp we had covering the trailer containing our only worldly possessions came loose so we had to pull off the road to fix the bungee cords and put it back on. We had hoped our escort would have noticed our dilemma and waited for us, but we lost him and had to make our own way to the Mexican border that night.

While driving into the first town we came to, it was late afternoon and the sun was shining so brightly through our windshield that Todd didn't see the big gap in the pavement as we started driving onto a bridge that crossed a river. The trailer hitch on our Belizean custom made trailer came off as a bolt came loose from the trailer, and the hitch detached from the trailer and came through the back window of our van! There was glass everywhere but thankfully no one was hurt. A couple of kind Belizean men saw what had happened and ran to help us get our trailer hitch back on the van so we could get going again. Night was approaching and we decided just to accept the advice of those we met along the way who pointed us in the direction of the Mexico border.

We eventually found the immigration office at the border and had our passports stamped on the Belizean side. We asked the attendant if a big, plain dressed Amish family had come through and they said yes, they had been through just an hour or so before us.

That brought us a little relief although we were driving into Mexico with no experience and no idea of where we were going.

In the darkness of night, as we slowly made our way over the border and into the Yucatan peninsula, we found our driver waving us down and flashing their headlights from the parking lot of a small hotel where they had chosen to stay for the night. It seemed like a miracle that we had found them! God was watching over us! It seemed as if we had just found the needle in a haystack! I had lost all hope of ever finding them.

A couple of times our trailer came unhooked as we drove over speed bumps at security checkpoints while going through villages and towns. Each time it was as if God provided the right people with the right equipment to help us resolve our problem. One time, our trailer came off again as we were going over a speed bump at a security checkpoint while we were attempting to get onto a major highway. We watched in utter disbelief as a man, that seemed to come out of nowhere with just the right piece of equipment necessary to help us reconnect the detached trailer to our van, came and tightened the bolt that kept coming loose. We all agreed that he must have been an angel sent by God. I will never forget our oldest son's response of disbelief as we watched the welcomed stranger as

he approached us, "Where did you come from?" he asked.   We

asked if we could give him something for helping us and he declined

and said, "God Bless You" as he turned and disappeared through the

lanes of traffic. Never again, on our over two thousand mile

journey, did our trailer hitch come loose.

As we encountered more vehicle problems, roadblocks and

other more minor setbacks in our travel through Mexico, I prayed

silently one evening. "Lord, why does this have to be so difficult?"

I heard an inner - very still - small voice immediately respond to my

complaint, "When you chose to follow Me, you didn't choose the

easy path." I was shocked by such a tender, rapid response to my

discontentment but I found immediate comfort in knowing that the

Lord's presence was with us in spite of our trials and He was guiding

us safely home.

We knew that traveling after dark in Mexico was very

dangerous so we had planned in advance to stop and find a hotel

before dusk each night. Unfortunately we unwillingly broke that

rule our very first night traveling through Mexico. Apparently there

was a "protest" of some sort and traffic was backed up for many miles. We were stuck and had no choice but to wait it out as the day

turned to darkness. The police were involved but we had no idea

how serious the incident was, so there was no reason to try to get

around the long line of vehicles.

Left to Right- Addie, Esther, Grace, Jenaya, Raven, Livia

Our second night in Mexico.

Thankfully our experienced travel companions knew enough

to carefully check the hotel rooms and mattresses beforehand for bed

bugs. I began to carefully intentionally watch my plain dressed

conservative sister in Christ with her adorable children as we made

our way through the hotel to our assigned rooms. Apart from her

long floor length dress and covered hair, I was drawn to her quiet, contented, submissive spirit. She possessed qualities I didn't have but longed to embrace. She had been sheltered from the world her entire life and I could tell. Christian virtues emulated from her being and her countenance radiated a peaceful glow. Without knowing it, she was mentoring me on this trip. Our oldest son spent some time talking with her husband and found out that they lived in a conservative Christian community in Caneyville, Kentucky. Before we parted ways at the United States Border, I made sure to get their phone number and address. I knew I would never forget them and we might want to contact them in the future and we did.

On our trip through the U.S. in route to Michigan, we took a detour to Tennessee to visit my oldest sister and a different "horse and buggy" conservative Christian community in Delano. We didn't find our friends whom we had met and spent time with at the Springfield community in Belize. Apparently they were out of town, but we did get the opportunity to meet George and Catherine. They had come "out of the world" also and seemed to recognize and identify with us. We were invited to stay for supper, an invitation I now regret declining, but before we left, Catherine gave us yummy snacks for our trip and a small publication by a man named Elmo

Stoll.   Later we found out that Elmo was a former Amish Bishop that walked away from the Amish Church and started Christian communities for those who were "seekers". Seekers were defined by Stoll as people coming out of the worldly apostate churches searching for truth. We identified with the writings of Elmo Stoll. We were the epitome of the title, "Upstream Pilgrims" having already made many of the steps he mentioned that seekers usually make during their spiritual journey. Our girls and I had turned all of our pants into skirts while living in Belize after our oldest adopted daughter, Adelyn, brought Deuteronomy chapter 22 verse 5 to our attention. *"A woman must not wear men's clothing nor a man wear women's clothing."*

I had not cut my hair for the nearly two years we were there and wore it up in a bun. We homeschooled our youngest eight children at the time and had decided not to send our second family of adopted children to public schools. We stopped watching television and we became convicted about the issue of head covering based on 1 Corinthians chapter 11. Amazingly, Elmo Stoll seemed to have written "our story" and the Conservative man whose young family we followed through Mexico. Ironically his name was Aaron Stoll, the eldest son of Elmo Stoll, the author of the publication that we had read after our Delano, Tennessee visit that we found to be so encouraging. Now I knew for sure that God was somehow engineering something in and through our circumstances. This was all much more than a mere coincidence.

After settling into our new home in Michigan the year following our return from Belize, we decided to go for a visit to see our Conservative Christian friends in Caneyville, Kentucky. Our oldest son had been living with them for a short time while working at their factory making wood cook stoves. While there, we met many other wonderful God fearing and God loving families in their isolated conservative community in the beautiful hills of southern Kentucky. We excitedly welcomed their "new to us" perspectives and teachings on Biblical life applications.

Chapter 8

Lessons In Vulnerability

"To be vulnerable is to voluntarily place yourself,

for the sake of a larger purpose,

in a situation that could bring pain."

(Strong Women, Soft Hearts by Paula Rinehart page 91)

Having walked away from churches filled with apostasy, we resigned to asking Jesus to be our teacher (Matt. 23:8) and committed to walk in His ways. One of the first topics of our personal deeper Biblical study became the subject of family size and the use of birth control. We studied the Bible principles and scriptures relating to the subject and also studied the origin of birth control and what we believed to be its Satanic purpose since God's

mandate to man was to "be fruitful and multiply" in Genesis 1:28.

Although we had 12 children at the time, in obedience we felt

compelled to repent for our decision to intentionally and

permanently prevent any more children. We had hoped for a rapid

reward for making restitution, but after a while it became apparent

that God was not in a hurry to increase our family size. After many

years of disappointments, I felt like God was telling me to stop

trying to control the situation. I was led to read the account of Sarah

in Genesis 18 over and over again. "I will give you a baby in your

old age. Is anything too hard for the Lord? With God all things are

possible." We felt at peace having decided to let God be God. We

were submitting our family planning to The Giver and Creator of all

life while making ourselves available to Him.

Fast forward, eight years later…My heart recognized this

stirring. I had experienced this feeling a number of times before.

Seven times to be exact. I dove into the Word, seeking, searching,

asking, praying, "Lord, direct our steps, I know there is someone

else that you desire to bring into our lives." We considered foster

care, foster to adopt, researched other international options, looked into the beginning stages of filling out applications, and we prayed. I looked into special needs adoptions and I prayed for orphans in China, Bulgaria, Ethiopia, Congo, and California. I looked at their precious little faces on online photo listings of children awaiting families. I questioned God, "Is it him? Is it her? Lord, who is it that might need us? Who are you stirring my heart for?" Secretly and silently I pursued God's will. He knows, like the parable of the widow before the unjust judge in Luke 18, I am persistent.

First, there was ten year old Norah. She captured my heart and my attention with her painful, insecure smile and her bare, shaved head, a possible result of a recent battle with head lice. She was ten years old living at an orphanage in Ethiopia, one of "These 400", a group of orphans through Bethany International Adoption Agency needing a home and a family of their own. Was this just my adoption bio clock ticking? Or was this God stirring my heart once again? We were approaching the "now or never" age of international adoption. We were told that Ethiopian adoption would be a high risk since their courts are not fond of large families. I surrendered and prayed for a family for my girl Norah. Our second oldest daughter told us about a special needs baby that had been abandoned at the

University of Michigan Children's hospital. She pleaded with us to

foster- to- adopt him. Our granddaughter had been born with similar

special needs and I had been trained in trach care and ventilator

support. With a heart full of compassion for this abandoned baby

boy, our daughter eagerly encouraged us to consider adopting this

special needs infant. Although I would have been willing to take

this unique challenge, it didn't feel as if that was what God was

calling us to do and Todd wasn't so sure that we could commit to 24

hour care of a handicapped child at our age while desiring to be

available, involved and supportive of our teenage children and

grandchildren as well.

One Sunday, we had a special speaker at church and I was so

sure he had been sent by God to deliver a message to my heart. I

intently listened as he frequently alluded to "our adoption by faith"

(Ephesians 1:5). Just hearing that word "adoption" repeatedly made

me anxious to hear more from God about our specific situation. I

came home from church somewhat frustrated. I began scouring

through scripture seeking a word from the Lord again when my six

lovely teenage daughters broke into three part harmony from the

kitchen singing, "There are no orphans, there are no outcasts, there are no orphans of God." "Ok Lord, This is too much! This must be more than my desire, this must be you I am hearing!" I began searching the world over for that precious one, and looked into the adoption requirements for many different countries. The only aspect we did not consider was domestic infant adoption. Impossible! Expensive! Too old! Never! It was not even something we would have nor never had, considered for all those various reasons and many more.

In pursuing another adoption, there seemed to be a few things that could be problematic for us:

- Our age (Todd 54, Noreen 52)

- Our family size (10 at the time)

- No insurance (other than church wide brotherhood assistance)

- Finances - no available resources for adoption expenses.

One day as I was reading through posts on an Anabaptist Christian adoption email support group that I had actively joined. I read that there were "opportunities" for newborn domestic adoption with an attorney that was looking for Christian families for unborn babies. We soon found out that she had a waiting list for baby girls, but these available placements were for baby boys. We were told

that this attorney was open to working with conservative Mennonites

and that she was willing to waive her initial fee! I very reluctantly

brought the idea of adopting a newborn infant to my husband and

explained to him the importance of connecting with the attorney as

soon as possible. To my shock, he agreed to look into it and agreed

to pray about it! I connected with the attorney the next day and she

laughed at every reason I threw at her that could possibly disqualify

us for domestic adoption. She even went so far as to give us the

contact info for an adoption agency in Grand Rapids, Michigan that

had worked with her in the past that would update our home study

for a very reasonable fee.

Before we walked too far into this journey it was of the

utmost importance that we made sure that this was God's will and

His desire, not just a desire of our own hearts. I listened intently to

my husband pray before leaving for work the next morning. I

resigned myself to my husband's authority and assumed it was all

over. He had gone too far in my opinion, and had set before God an

impossible fleece. There was no taking back what spilled forth from

his mouth in prayer, and he was serious. "Lord, we can't take steps in this adoption until we know that this is of you. If you want us to

go forward with this, then please send someone to make a cash offer

on our old house today." That last word, that word "today" was

certainly the clincher. We had had our old Beaverton farmhouse for

sale for nearly a year and we had not had one reasonable cash offer

yet. Interestingly, I felt at peace and found myself agreeing with

him in prayer, "Yes, Lord," although I was in a state of unbelief and

had not any hope of his "impossible" request being granted that day.

Surely this request, in my opinion, would no doubt be "too hard for

the Lord". I went about my day while trying to put the opportunity

in front of us out of my mind. Within a few hours, around 11AM

that same morning, I got a shocking text message from someone who

had been interested in our house many months prior but had never

actually manifested any serious offer. His exact words, "I would

like to make a cash offer on your house." My stomach took a

nauseous turn as if I were experiencing some extreme serious

morning sickness. I nearly fell to my knees as I literally cried out to

God in tears, "This IS of you!" Surely I was being taught that

NOTHING IS IMPOSSIBLE WITH GOD. Maybe not in the exact

way we had originally expected, but yes, we WERE going to have a baby in our old age just as I had felt led to believe so many years prior.

I immediately got in touch with Todd and he too was impressed and amazed with God's rapid answer to his fleece that same morning. We both rejoiced knowing that this was an open door invitation and that God seemed to be encouraging us to pursue this domestic infant adoption. The purpose in asking God for the sale of our home, was for the provision of paying off a debt that needed to be taken care of before we could ever begin to consider another adoption. The finances for the adoption itself would be another matter entirely, but as we fervently sought to "test and approve God's good, pleasing and perfect will" in this situation, we knew He would give us the resources for that as well. We intimately had come to know Jehovah- Jireh, as our provider having experienced God's hand of provision many times in what seemed to be miraculous, unexpected ways. While still early in the process, our faith was rewarded in the form of an unexpected check that was large enough to fund the adoption minus travel expenses. The Lord was quickly moving on our behalf at every turn!

One Sunday morning at church as I prayed, I wrote in my journal while taking notes, "Lord, help my unbelief." It seemed as if the Lord was opening doors, yet I was so afraid to allow myself to feel the joy of this wonderful possibility. Surely I did not want to be presumptuous and become too confident should this all turn out to be just some crazy, conjured up idea we made up in our heads. After church, I was talking to another sister when her sweet blond haired seven year old daughter Tanisha handed me a craft she had made in Sunday school that morning. It was a cut out of her own handprint with the scripture from John 20:29: "Blessed are they that have not seen and yet have believed." I was beyond overwhelmed. The Lord speaks through His word to His children. This was surely more than just a coincidence. Out of the 31,102 verses in the King James Bible, I get handed a verse that speaks directly to the prayer of my heart just moments prior? Only God knew what I had written in my journal that very morning! Surely this was encouragement from the Lord Himself. No human being knew the thoughts and meditations of my heart, nor did they know what verse would have the power to conquer my doubts and fears! Over the following days and months,

I frequently looked at that hand with that verse as a wonderful

symbol of God's divine encouragement.

I gathered my courage and decided to call Char Lanning,

Executive Director of Families through Adoption, the social worker

from the agency in Grand Rapids, Michigan that our attorney had

recommended. As I began to go through my list of concerns with

her, she too laughed at me! "I adopted my youngest baby when I

was 53 years old. Oh, I am aware of brotherhood assistance, I have

worked with the Amish. No insurance? That's not a problem. There

are no family size laws disqualifying you for domestic adoption."

All concerns addressed, all green lights, all open doors! Now I could

check off obstacles 1 - 3 ! Wait! Maybe just one snag. "You must

prove all your children are healthy and up to date with

immunizations." Healthy? Yes. Up to date? No. In our search for "truth" as upstream pilgrims we had started to seriously question the ingredients and negative side effects of vaccines. We decided we would continue to walk by faith and fill out waivers, which we believed was still a legal option. At the very beginning of our home study process, this subject became very concerning to Char, our social worker. There was a big national scare over a recent measles outbreak at that time. Todd was determined that we would stand on our personal convictions and not compromise. His reply to my willingness to cave in to her demands was, "If we don't stand for something, we will fall for anything." I respected his firm convictions. In response to our social workers request that we vaccinate the children to appease whatever concern the judge may have, I suggested that I would contact our attorney and seek her professional opinion on whether the judge would have a problem with our convictions on vaccinating. To my delight, I got a quick short email reply from our attorney. She told us that it should not be a problem, that we were within the law and still had the right not to vaccinate. In addition, I was thrilled when she told me that she agreed with our decision! I was so excited to take this information back to our social worker! She never mentioned the issue again.

We strategically went about preparing for our physical exams as supporting documents for our home study report. Todd had had a history of high blood pressure, although by watching his diet he was able to bring it down to a normal range and had decided not to stay on medication. It had been a while since he had had it checked, so we went to work on improving our diet and taking specific supplements to help regulate his blood pressure. One evening while shopping at WalMart, I suggested that he go to the pharmacy section and have his BP taken by the machine there. He came back with a very unsatisfactory report of an extremely high reading and was sure that the machine was not working properly. The following week I took all six of our girls in for their physicals and then it was Todd's turn to take the boys. We had prayed and prayed that God would do a work and that Todd would pass his exam without any issues. After their physicals, I got a text message from Todd that simply said: 128/80. NO WAY! His BP had never come close to that in years even with medication! Surely God had done this for us to show forth his power and we praised him for it!

"Delight thyself also in the Lord

and He shall give thee the desires of thine heart.

Commit your way to the LORD, Trust also in Him,

and He shall bring it to pass."

Psalm 37:5

I had known the pain of rejection as a few friends and family members had opposed our calling during previous adoptions. It was not an experience I would choose to repeat, but here we were again, willing to be vulnerable, intentionally having to risk rejection, allowing God the opportunity to strip more precious friendships away from my life knowing from past experience that not everyone understands and approves of our mission and calling in life. Only now we were dealing with different concerns, different circumstances and different friends. How could I expect others to comprehend what God was doing when I didn't fully understand it myself? I carefully chose to confide in one friend from church. I felt like I NEEDED to tell someone what God was doing just to confirm it in my own mind and she seemed like a safe person. Just as I anticipated, she was thrilled by our new news and encouragement flowed from her sweet spirit. After a short time had lapsed, it was necessary that I build the courage to tell a larger audience.

Developing the virtue of courage required me to step even farther out of my comfort zone. Surely my closest sisters needed to hear this story from me and not from another source. Four of us ladies from church had been enjoying a wonderful Bible study together and since it seemed we had all been growing spiritually and drawing closer together through our study, I felt that I needed to start with them. It was incredibly hard to articulate what was in my mind and on my heart without floods of emotion spilling out. I had no idea what their reaction would be and I was extremely nervous and scared to find out. Soon, there were three of us crying together in my living room and one desperately trying to make sense of it all. I could see the familiar look of disapproval and suddenly I was staring my own fear of rejection in the face. Ironically, I noticed one of the other ladies was also frequently checking the fallen countenance of my disapproving friend, which just solidified my thoughts. No, I wasn't just being over sensitive. My two faith story supporters were very certain that God was writing this adoption story and questioned how anyone could doubt it with all the answered prayers and open doors? Then there was the third sister who immediately and bluntly let me know that women are supposed to stop having children at the age of forty. I'm still not aware of any Biblical basis for her belief. I had just spent eight years meditating on what God had to say about one hundred year old Abraham and ninety year old Sarah's experience.   And surely God did not have to wait until Elizabeth was approximately 89, well past the age of child bearing, before He blessed her with a son. Maybe He wanted to show and teach the world that "With God, ALL things are possible." Luke 1: 37

While I was determined to submit to whatever God had planned for this baby, my husband and my children seemed more convinced than I that God had already chosen us to be his family. When we hit some bumps in the home study road, it was our sixteen year old daughters, Livia and Raven that voluntarily fasted and prayed. There were many days and weeks that I couldn't even consider preparing for a baby; I was too busy trying to protect my own heart from all the uncertainties. But frequently I found our Livia in the nursery sorting and looking through the used baby clothing we had gathered while quietly praying, seeking and believing God for the arrival of her new baby brother. What a precious sight to see her faith being tested in the same way ours had

been tested for her adoption thirteen years previously.

A fleeting prayer crossed my mind and my lips as I slid out

of our 2001 E350, 12 passenger van one morning. Our big full size

van had been totaled the previous year when my husband slid on

black ice and rolled it into a ditch. The damage would have cost

more to repair than what the van was worth yet it still ran like a

charm so we kept driving it in spite of its looks. Only now, the

engine was beginning to have some trouble and our twelve year old

van was nearly ready to retire.

Having just been matched with our new expectant birth

parents, we didn't trust that our old van could possibly make an

impending journey to Arkansas and I cringed at the thought of the

possibility of putting a newborn passenger in it!   Not long after, we

got a call one evening from our special friends in Texas. "We know

that you have a need for a new van, we would ship one to you but it

might be better if you shop for one there in Michigan and we will

send you the funds." We tried to contain our emotions! God was

supplying our need once again! I truly don't remember if I had

shared my concerns about our van with our dear friends, or if the

Holy Spirit inspired them to help us with the van, but in either case, we believe it was God working through them to fulfill our need!

One evening we gathered the children for devotions and set out to confirm their thoughts on adopting a new sibling. The boys maintained their joy a bit better than some of the girls! They were all delighted! In subsequent evenings we poured over baby names as a family. Todd would read through lists as we had fun rejecting or embracing each name. One night, he came to the name "Calum" meaning "DOVE- MESSENGER OF PEACE". For some reason it stood out for several of us and we pondered it as a strong possibility. Further down the alphabetical list was "Gavriel", a Hebrew name meaning "GOD IS MY STRENGTH". A very special name for a very special gift from God.

One day I went to my prayer closet to expose my heart's struggle with my wavering unbelief once again. I opened a book of adoption testimonies to a story written by Marie Keller, a mother of several children adopted from China. The title of her story was "The Price of Ransom". "You have never tested the resources of God until you have attempted the humanly impossible." My heart resonated with her testimony as she explained the reason for their adoptions - "to ransom another soul". For so long "this" adoption

didn't make sense to me. I understood the "rescuing" of orphans in

their distress, I understood the pure religion of visiting the fatherless,

but weren't infant domestic adoptions reserved for young, childless

couples? Now I had a greater understanding of God's purpose - To

bring Glory to God, to show His power in our weakness, to "ransom

a soul" and introduce him to our Lord and Savior. Who was I or

anyone else to be questioning God's motives anyway? Maybe there

are just some things we may never know and may never understand.

Maybe simply trusting God and believing Him is enough. Like

those who were contrary to this adoption, I too questioned and could

not grasp why God would be choosing us for this purpose. But my

soul rejoiced that He did!

After a concerning phone call from the doctor's office in

Arkansas proclaiming the possibility of a sooner than expected birth

of our soon-to-be adopted son, our social worker began writing our

home study as I dictated answers to her questions. We got through

most of our interviews and questions and then Char said she needed

to call our four grown adult children to interview them that evening

to ask if they approved of the adoption. The next call I received from her was strained and I could tell she was struggling to grasp the real picture. Her tone had suddenly changed with me and I could sense something was wrong. She asked me to go to a room where I would be alone. Then she proceeded to give me a list of what apparently seemed to her like impossible requests. The first item of concern was supposed to break me, I think. She calmly let me know that our income did not meet the government poverty guidelines and that we were $5,000 short of meeting the annual income for a family of our size, which totaled ten people living at home. As she listened to my casual response she seemed shocked that I wasn't devastated by the bad news. "No, I'm not surprised. This is just an obstacle that God will move on our behalf "IF" this adoption is His will." I reminded her that I truly believed that if God initiated this adoption, then it would be up to Him to finish it. By now we had had enough confirmation to know these were merely mountains we must climb and obstacles to overcome but certainly not closed doors. I also explained to her that every adoption has literally cost us blood, sweat and tears. Adoption is not for the faint of heart and whoever first said it, wasn't kidding. Then the rest came tumbling out....

Four grown adult children and two very different and interesting perspectives. I had warned Char about two of our oldest children's less than favorable opinions, but she was not prepared for their seemingly legitimate concerns that suddenly caused her faith in us to waiver. We had two adult children expressing their approval by saying that we were gifted with children and that we were very involved in the lives of our children and grandchildren. Then we had another adult child sharing that we weren't even taking care of the children we already had. Ironically, it was this adult child's idea that we adopt the medically fragile baby boy that had been abandoned at the University of Michigan hospital just a couple of months prior. As a single mom, we had been helping this daughter raise her two oldest children since they were newborn babies.

Systematically, we documented proof of our parental capabilities and of our ongoing participation and involvement in the lives of our children and grandchildren. We submitted several more articles in which we were asked to write showing what we had learned from our son's placement in residential care at Cal Farley Boys Ranch in Amarillo, Texas for behavioral and emotional issues. These articles had to express what we had learned since his release, why we chose to have him released, who we would like for our

children to marry, our goals for our children, etc., etc. etc. Noah's

placement for attachment issues suddenly became a highlighted

subject and Char let us know that if we couldn't get all the additional

necessary documents she needed prior to the baby being born, then

we could talk to the attorney about getting on the waiting list for a

different match (baby). My heart screamed inside of me,

"NOOOOOO!" But thankfully the Lord helped me keep my

composure and control my tongue as I calmly expressed to her that

that would not be an option for us. Todd had already adamantly

stated that if this adoption did not work out that we were done and

we would not pursue another. I explained also that we were

developing a wonderful, trusting and loving relationship with our

expecting birth parents and that we did not want to let them down or

lose their trust. Unlike the normally passive person that I considered

myself to be, I aggressively let Char know that we would not be

backing out of this one and go on to another. She didn't understand,

like so many others, that this adoption was not just a pursuit of a

baby as much as it was a pursuit of God and His will for all of us.

Article after article, I wrote and wrote and wrote until Char was appeased with our parenting ability, our emotional and spiritual growth in overcoming the effects of being raised by alcoholic parents, our goals for our children, our understanding of attachment issues, and most importantly our reasons for placing Noah and getting professional help for his issues. I confessed to Char that I had become an enabler. I had been overextending myself and had allowed two of our adult children to use me. I was doing things for them that they should have been doing for themselves. We had developed an unhealthy codependent relationship and what we were now experiencing were the consequences of walking away from their unhealthy expectations. Therefore this adoption of a newborn infant seemed to be a real possible threat to the family dynamic as it was.

As we set out to conquer the new list of additional requirements, we tackled one obstacle after another. The biggest one seemed to be the financial requirement, although we felt certain that God had the answer to this one for sure, since He does own the cattle on a thousand hills! We know He has access to whatever we need and He is more than able to provide it when we seek Him by faith.

The following day while at work, Todd went to his employer, who was also a brother in Christ from our home church. After sharing our problem of not meeting the poverty guidelines for a family of our size, his employer immediately - without reservation - asked Todd how much we needed. Amazingly and miraculously Todd walked out of work that day with a new employment letter for our home study documentation that included a $5,000 annual bonus! Only a man after God's own heart who has the ability to sense God at work would feel immediately led to do such a thing! What else could we do but praise the Giver of every good and every perfect gift!

"And my God will meet all your need

according to the riches of His glory in Christ Jesus."

Philippians 4:19

The list of required documents for every adoption includes a local police clearance and also federal fingerprinting. While at our adoption agency for a meeting, Char put me on her computer to fill out our applications for fingerprinting appointments. We realized then that Addie, our eighteen year old daughter still living at home, would also need police clearance and fingerprinting since she was now legally an adult. One big red flag went up when they said we would all need a photo ID. Addie had not yet gotten her driver's license. The following day, we went to the Secretary of State office to see about getting a state photo ID card. They gave a temporary ID without the photo and told us the new one would come in 2-3 weeks! Yikes! Our fingerprinting appointment was the following week. By faith we went anyway. In reading the directions on our applications, we noted that it is a federal law that everyone who is fingerprinted must show a photo identification card. At the counter I presented our applications and one by one she took us to the computer station where we would be fingerprinted. I went first, then Addie. When they asked for her ID, Addie gave them the temporary proof of her state ID without the photo. They asked her for a photo ID and Addie explained that she didn't have one. I could hardly believe my ears when the one doing our fingerprinting said, "Oh well, we trust you." I withheld my composure although I wanted to jump and shout "HALLELUJAH!!" We were originally told that fingerprinting would cost $84 per person. With three of us, that was a big expense, but when we got to the office to have our

fingerprinting done, they told us that the fingerprinting would cost

$54 per person. "Oh wow, that would be a savings and a blessing," I

thought to myself. After Todd and I and Addie were fingerprinted,

the attendant told us we were done. Then we asked about the

payment. "It shows on our computer that your fees have already

been paid," she said. I explained that there must be some mistake,

we had been told by our adoption agency to be prepared to pay for

the fingerprinting fees. The attendant went on to say, "We cannot

accept payment since it shows that payment has already been made.

Does your agency have an expense account?" I told her that I didn't

think so since our social worker was the one who told us to be

prepared to pay the fees at the time of the fingerprinting! We

walked away with receipts showing full payment for our

fingerprinting with the intention of figuring it all out later. I called

our social worker the next day and told her what had happened.

"No, we don't have an expense account," she said. It was a great

mystery to both of us now. "They will catch that mistake when they

process our prints," I decided. Interestingly, mysteriously and

maybe miraculously, our fingerprints were processed and cleared without ever knowing how they were paid for. To God Be the Glory! Great Things He Has Done! All requirements were now accomplished and everything was in order as far as it depended on us.

On March 23rd at about 2:30 pm, I got a call from Todd while he was at work. He had just heard from Calum's birth dad, Willow. He called to say that Malynna was in labor and they would be going to the hospital. Willow and Todd decided that Malynna should go to the hospital and make sure she was in active labor before we ventured out for our fourteen hour journey. I asked Todd if he could possibly come home and shower so we could be ready just in case. I felt a little numb. "Lord, what is happening? Are you really the author of this story? Are they going to change their minds once they deliver and see this precious babe? Are we going to be wounded, hurt, ashamed to have foolishly followed in this path, falsely believing and trusting that this was your will? Will Calum's birth parents accept us?" So many unanswered questions that required pure, BLIND FAITH. We had heard so many stories, truly heart wrenching stories of birth moms changing their minds and adoptive parents returning home with empty car seats and empty arms. It happens all the time. For this reason we opted to leave our children in the capable hands of some of our closest friends from church and go with the intention of supporting this family in whatever way they needed us.

"Whether you turn to the right or to the left,

your ears will hear a voice behind you, saying,

"This is the way; walk in it."

Isaiah 30:21

It was an agonizing yet exciting time of last minute preparations before we finally left our home in Michigan at 9:30 PM in route to Springdale, Arkansas. It felt like we were living a dream, so unsure of the events that would soon unfold. We communicated frequently with Willow on my cell phone and he kept us updated on the labor progress. Todd and I took turns attempting sleep and driving through the night. Thankfully at 5:30 am, just before daylight, Todd was driving when Calum's birth dad called one last time. "She is ready to push now," he said in a loud whisper. Before I had a chance to respond, he put the phone on speaker so we could hear the conversation in the room as the nurse encouraged Calum's mother to push one last time. Soon we heard the joyous sound of Calum's first cry. Tears flowed and joy filled my soul. Oh, the miracle of a new birth! Even though we were yet 6 hours away, we felt connected as if we had just been personally invited to share in the most precious and intimate experience of this child's delivery. I couldn't thank Calum's birth dad enough for thinking to do that for us. It was an experience I will never forget.

By 11:30 AM we arrived at the hospital, too full of excitement and apprehension to feel even slightly tired. Thankfully I had to use the restroom, so I had a reason to privately take a deep breath in solitude while shedding some more tears and surrendering the outcome of the day to the Lord in prayer before we went to meet our new family members. We were led down a hallway not knowing our first stop was to be at the nursery window. I saw two babies in isolates, and had no idea which one was Calum. We could see our attorney beyond the glass windows on the opposite side of the nursery at the nurse's desk going over paperwork. After several minutes that seemed like hours, a nurse finally wheeled Calum to the window for us to see. We couldn't take our eyes off of him. I was somewhat happy with the fact that he was in the nursery as if he was

waiting there for us. After all the hospital paperwork was

accomplished, our attorney came out to greet us. She took us first to

meet Calum's birth mother. She quickly introduced us to let her

know we were there. She had been sleeping and appeared very

groggy from her long night of labor, but she was absolutely radiantly

beautiful to me. Todd and I took turns hugging her and through

more tears, explained that we wanted her to sleep and we would

come back later. We were then led to a bench in the hospital

hallway to sign some important paperwork regarding the court date

and adoption finalization. I still kept waiting for the moment that the

big door would slam shut and we would walk away empty handed.

"Ah ha!" I thought to myself. "What paperwork? Will this be the

end of the line for us now that we are here?" Painlessly, our

attorney walked us through the remainder of the process. She told us

what the court fee would be for our finalization and she explained

that the birth parents would have a five day revocation period in

which they could decide to parent the baby, which we had already

been made aware of. She scheduled our court date for the following

week. Over and over in my mind I could scarcely believe that what was happening was real. Was God actually blessing us with a

beautiful baby boy? A nurse then came and showed us to our private

room where we would have the baby all to ourselves, and where we

would be allowed to spend the night with Calum before his release

the next day. Then, we went to go to see him and hold him for the

first time in Malynna's room where they had taken him. I was a bit

uncomfortable as the nurse explained to us how we should have skin

to skin contact with the baby for bonding purposes in front of

Willow and Malynna. I watched Malynna as she smiled sweetly at

Calum and put a new onesie on her newborn baby. I couldn't help

but wonder what she was thinking and if she just might decide to

keep him. I certainly wouldn't have blamed her if she did. Yet I was

well aware of their appropriate reasons for making this adoption plan

for their baby.

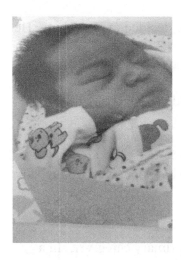

Calum Gavriel - 1 Day Old

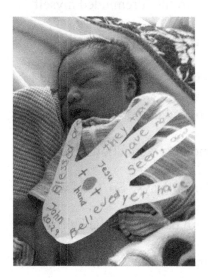

Calum

Willow seemed quite happy and relaxed with us and

immediately encouraged us to hold the baby. Todd went first and I

could see it was love at first sight. As Todd cuddled the tiny bundle in his big arms, Willow asked me what we decided to name him. He seemed pleased at the sound of "Calum Gavriel". After my turn at holding Calum, we were told that we could take the baby to our room whenever we were ready. It seemed so strange as my heart tried to decipher what was taking place. This poor sweet young lady just gave birth and here I am, wheeling her baby into another hospital room where I would become his primary caregiver. In a perfect world this would be oh so very wrong. I reminded myself that the decision to place this baby for adoption was theirs, not mine.

Before we left the room, I was given a hospital wristband to show who I was and that this baby belonged to me. I was instructed that only adoptive mothers and birth mothers were allowed to push the babies in their cart beds through the hallways. So Todd walked along beside me as I pushed our newborn baby down the hall. An older nurse came up behind me, smiling and said. "Aw, Grandma's got the baby!" I corrected her kindly by saying, "No, I'm the mom," while recalling that, if I were the grandmother, I should have been scolded for breaking the rules! I was sure this was just the first of many same assumptions and I would simply need to get used to it.

Our brief twenty- four hour hospital stay was a true blessing. We enjoyed a pizza supper with Calum's birth family in Malynna's room. We met Calum's maternal grandparents, older siblings and a few extended family members. This family amazingly embraced us and clearly supported Calum's bio parents in this decision without any reservations. Prior to us all being discharged together the next day, we were asked to join the family for a relative's birthday party the following Friday night.

While traveling to the birthday celebration, I was struggling with thoughts of what the evening could bring. We understood that this was going to be a huge event with possibly 100-200 people. It would be the first time Calum's birth parents would see him since we were all discharged from the hospital. We still had three days to go before the revocation period was over. Would they choose to take him home tonight? I was walking into one of the most vulnerable situations I could ever imagine- "risking my heart…willing to be hurt". As Todd drove through the rain, I took in the sights of the unfamiliar city. A mattress store sign had a large, brightly lit banner sign that caught my attention. I could hardly believe my eyes as we drove past. In big bold red letters, it said,

GOD….. IS….. IN….. CONTROL…... "Really God, a mattress store sign!? Did you put that there for me?" Peace swept over my heart as I realized the truth in the message. It wasn't an audible voice or idea, it was more like a knowing. "It doesn't matter who takes the baby home tonight. Your job is to trust Me and know that in all your circumstances, I AM." I could feel His gentle prodding, "Love ME more than my gifts." God has promised over and over in His word that if we pray according to His will that we shall receive whatever we ask in prayer. (Matthew 21: 22)

As we completely surrendered our all to the will of our Heavenly Father, making sure that first and foremost, HE was the ultimate desire of our hearts, (Psalm 37: 4-5) THEN He was free to give us the desires of our hearts because in surrendering, HIS desire BECAME our desire. Sometimes that can even mean becoming the mother of a newborn adopted baby boy at the age of 52 years old.

Sometime later I pondered God's wisdom in using a mattress store sign to show me what seemed to be a message from heaven. Where do you go for a physical rest? A mattress! Where do you go for spiritual rest? Jesus Christ! "Come unto me all ye that labor and are heavy laden and I will give you REST." (Matthew 11:28) My heart was so heavy as we headed to that birthday party that night, and through God's message in those few simple words, my faith was restored. I was at peace; my heart and my mind were "at rest".

Now I understand that looking for "signs" is what pagans do and not what Christians should be doing. We can't just look to the stars or rainbows or mattress store signs for guidance and call it God's will for our lives. I realize that we must be so in tune with the Lord, so continuously connected in prayer, so closely abiding in Him and so surrendered to HIS will that we aren't led astray by seeking signs as confirmation or reasons to pursue any sort of direction for our lives.

The party was a wonderful event, full of Pacific island traditions, food and family. We felt loved and accepted from the start. We were introduced to more family than we could remember. It was obvious that this adoption was a welcomed arrangement with this family. I encouraged Malynna to hold Calum and she reluctantly did. I truly wanted her to be confident in her choice to place him with us. Grandma and an Auntie passed the baby around our table as they took turns admiring him. It was amazing how trusting and accepting this family was. I felt the love of Christ through them and I wondered what in the world are we missing? Have we become so judgmental that we scorn others who live differently than we do or who make choices that we necessarily wouldn't make? It felt as if these people had something to teach us. All I could think about was a recent sermon we had just heard about "the sin of being a respecter of persons." I felt that familiar feeling of being on a missions trip when you think you are going to go spread the gospel, change the world, feed the hungry, clothe the naked, make a difference and return with a greater sense of humility realizing that these people have a contentment and a joy while living in the midst of suffering that I can hardly comprehend.

For the next few days we stayed in a hotel in Springdale bonding with Calum. He was a joy to our souls. We couldn't have loved him more if he had just been born to us. We felt God's presence throughout our stay and never doubted that we were right where God wanted us at the time, regardless of the outcome.

Before leaving the birthday party on Saturday evening, we made plans with Calum's birth parents to meet for a Chinese dinner on Monday prior to our court date on Tuesday. As Todd and I tried to manipulate the timing, planning for dinner reservations after the revocation period which would end at 5pm that day, Calum's birth family decided that they wanted to meet sooner. My heart was sick. We would be standing in the final moments of many months of unknowns. I would have preferred not to be exactly "with" them during those last minutes of time when they could suddenly decide to parent their baby. I love Chinese food, but I could barely eat. I tried, but my meal was far from enjoyable. My heart was anguishing. I could hardly feel happy about our precious blessing knowing that our gain was their pain. Malynna seemed distant and she stayed busy distracting herself with her cell phone throughout most of our celebration dinner. Willow and all the little siblings adored us and baby Calum.

Before parting ways, Todd and I both shed some tears as we thanked them for choosing life for Calum and for entrusting him to us. We spent some time taking family group pictures and sharing our thankfulness for one another. Slowly I started to relax and feel the joyous merging of two cultures and two families as the maternal grandparents placed Malaysian tokens of respect around our necks; large necklaces made with shells and dried palm leaves from the islands. The sober look on their faces helped me to know that this adoption was solidified in their hearts and minds. They trusted us.

We experienced a deep mutual respect that exceeded my greatest

expectations in spite of language and cultural barriers. Our family

had just increased by many more than just one that day. My heart

rejoiced, my cup was overflowing.

Tuesday, March 31, 2015, our sweet baby Calum was seven

days old when we walked into the courthouse. It was a very hot and

humid day in Arkansas. A kindhearted police officer offered to

"babysit" our baby while we went through the security detectors. To

my embarrassment, my hair pins set off the alarm. I offered to

remove them, but they quickly decided that that wouldn't be

necessary and let us go on through. Up on the 3rd floor, we waited

to enter the Judge's chambers as our attorney went through our

documents one last time. I was surprised by the short, informal

meeting we had with the Judge alone in her chambers. She appeared

to be quite young and expressed a great interest in our family and

our previous adoptions. Unknown to me, our attorney pulled out a

full size enlargement of our family photo for the Judge to see. She

started asking questions about our Liberian and Haitian adoptions.

The atmosphere was warm and friendly. The Judge not only

approved, she was extremely excited about our adoptions. At the stroke of her gavel, having previously reviewed our home study and supporting documents, Calum Gavriel Weaver was officially pronounced our son as I fought back tears of gratitude and great relief. Taking pictures was in order and the Judge took her place beside me, smiling with much enthusiasm. She told us that this was the only fun part of her job.

We met with Calum's birth family for a farewell dinner one last time the night before we left to travel home. Whatever anxiety I had had before was gone now that the legal aspect had been taken care of and we were now officially Calum's adoptive parents. I immensely enjoyed our visit and saying good-bye was harder than I had anticipated. It seemed as if we had adopted a whole family and a new culture, in addition to our sweet baby boy.

"To one who has faith, no explanation is necessary.

To one without faith no explanation is possible."

(Source unknown)

Calum Gavriel Weaver- Two years old

Chapter 9

Numero Catorce

"Behold children are a gift of the Lord"

Psalm 127:3-5

We sat on polished wooden benches in the hallway as we waited our turn to go into the Judge's chambers. We had sat in this same exact place just eight months prior. The last time we were there this place was empty and no one else was waiting to see a Judge. This time we had to squeeze in to find a seat. As I looked around I could only imagine what choice or decision had all these people made that had brought us all together there that day. Out of the crowd, I believe Todd and I may have been the only ones that were happy to be there. I saw an older, balding man bent over in his seat and holding his head in his hands, obviously not feeling very well about his position in life at that moment. I overheard an attorney explaining something to one woman about the "document of divorce" and my heart sank and grieved for her. Choices we had made brought us all to this one place for so many different reasons. "Mr. Sanchez?" an attorney in a dark gray suit greeted a man across from us with his outstretched hand. "Your hearing is postponed until we can get a court appointed translator, do you understand?" The dark haired Mr. Sanchez nodded his head, "Si".

Decisions and choices, our lives are full of them every day. Just forty-five days prior, we were in a position to make a difficult decision. We could accept the offer to adopt a baby boy to be born in the following six weeks or we could have declined and let the opportunity go. As always, we went to the Lord to seek His will for this child and for us. We had to determine whether we should walk into this by faith or whether possibly God had another plan.

For several months since Calum's adoption it had been discussed among our immediate family at home that Calum could not be an "only child". There was a thirteen year age gap between Esther, our youngest daughter and Calum. Everyone seemed to feel as if there was still a "someone" missing even though our hearts were bursting at the seams with love and gratitude for our beautiful sweet baby Calum. Having a mother and six big sisters doting on baby Calum alone was beginning to look like a disaster waiting to happen. He needed someone to share all this attention with or this was going to be one very spoiled little boy. One day, two of the girls were joking back and forth and they made a comment, "You know what? We are like the s'more family! Ya, Mom and Dad are the marshmallows, we (all eight of the oldest children at home) are the chocolate and Calum is the graham cracker! We just need one more graham cracker!" (I'm sure in their innocence they did not realize the political incorrectness of their remarks. Please do not take offense.)

Our attorney knew that we had thoughts of a future adoption and that we had considered adopting another precious one to raise for the Lord. We had already been offered two babies to be born in the month of November. After rejecting the first two, not being sure of this timing, we decided to consider the third opportunity. We realized that if we adopted again now instead of waiting we wouldn't need to start over with our home study, we could just do a quick amendment to our existing one that had not yet expired. An open door opportunity was in front of us.

The baby was due in six short weeks. The expecting mother was just released from a six month jail term and she was asking for a "closed" adoption meaning no contact and no shared personal information. This was the extreme opposite from our last "open" adoption experience with Calum. She was choosing to not even see the baby after her scheduled cesarean birth, and she seemed quite determined to stick with her adoption plan according to our attorney. We were told that the baby's biological father was forced to surrender his rights when he was deported back to Mexico due to some illegal activity.

Although we had exhausted all our financial resources with Calum, we knew that "if" this adoption was God's will He would provide once again. By faith, we didn't need to see evidence of where it would come from. Immediately I got to work on all I knew to do. Grace had turned eighteen during the year so I knew she would need fingerprinting and a police clearance. Calum was new to our family since the home study for his adoption, so he would need to have a recent physical form which was simple since he had just had his six month checkup the month before. I called and left a

message for our social worker about our need for an update. This

proved to be our first stumbling point. She was leaving for a long

trip out of the country and she told me we would need to start over

with another agency. Zealous to accomplish this goal within a

couple weeks, I started searching for an agency that would help us. I

had a conscious understanding that starting over would require much

more time and we might need to plan an extended stay in Arkansas

awaiting the home study document to be sent by mail. After making

my first attempt, I found another agency that agreed to work with us.

Between our attorney and our previous social worker from our last

agency, I communicated often. Finally all misunderstandings aside,

I got a call from Char. "Noreen, I am calling to apologize to you. I

did not realize that your home study was less than one year old. I

can write an amendment to the current study and it should only take

2-3 weeks." Hallelujah!! But then she warned us of another

possible snare. The State of Michigan was merging with another

company and the fingerprinting was backed up for several weeks.

There would be no issuing a new updated home study without the

proof of Grace's fingerprinting clearance. I felt little or no concern.

We were determined to do what we could do and leave the rest up to God. Having Char change her mind and agree to work with us was a huge encouragement to me that God was working in this adoption. We saw evidence of God's favor also when I took Grace for her fingerprinting and police clearance. Once again, just like with our previous experience, there was "no charge" as the computer printed her receipt as if it had already been paid. Then again, when I took her for her police clearance letter, what took three weeks the last time, took approximately thirty minutes this time. All seemed to be going well but there was still this mountain of the adoption expense and the Lord still had not shown us where it was going to come from. Our short span of time was running out before the attorney was asking for a commitment and an initial payment toward the adoption fees. Surely the Lord would have to do something if this was His will for us. Without even realizing fully how our faith was being tested, we laid our baby boy on the altar and surrendered him before the Lord. I went to our adoption support group and "advertised" for another family that was home study approved and financially ready to step in and take over our adoption opportunity. It didn't feel right and it went against everything inside of me that screamed, "This is MY baby!!" but we were running out of time and we felt forced to surrender. I got responses from three families who were excited about this possibly being "their" baby also. So now it was up to me to choose from these? I wasn't comfortable with making that kind of decision. My only concern was that a Christian family stepped into our shoes. Then a different sort of response came from my desperate plea. Someone seemed to realize the pain I was experiencing and suddenly God provided a ram in the bush. Apparently this kind soul did not believe that money should be the reason to pull away from this adoption. At the same time we had started sharing our need in the form of a true prayer request with our very small closest group of friends (in addition to our adoption support group), we were blessed with a gift and a loan that totaled the required initial adoption fee. Within 24 hours we received additional financial gifts and offers of loans to fund the entire adoption from some people of which we didn't even know personally. When my husband got home from work the next day, I was on the phone with someone I did not know and had never met. When I got off the phone I shared with him how this woman was calling from another state offering their financial help with our adoption. Tears streamed down his face as he silently stared out our living room picture window in awe of God's goodness and faithfulness to provide. I remembered his prayer from the previous night; "Lord, we can't make this happen and we don't want to try to make this happen. Lord, if this is YOUR will, we need you to provide." I can only imagine that the relief we felt was in some very small way similar to how Abraham felt upon seeing the ram in the bush after he had placed Isaac on the altar.

One day I received a call from our attorney, warning us that our expecting mother was showing signs of early labor. We debated as to whether to stay and wait it out until we got the call or whether we should go and be sure to be there for the birth. Again we were fourteen hours away and a c-section takes on average one hour from start to finish. Knowing the biological mother did not want to see her baby after the birth, we felt moved to be there for the baby when he was born. His scheduled due date was November 12th. We left November 4th and made the road trip from Michigan to Arkansas. We had no choice but to leave without our completed home study which could honestly have been labeled as stupidly presumptuous on our part!

Waiting was hard, but yet easier since we were so much closer to our soon- to- be- born son. The days turned into a week and still no baby. We excitedly packed the baby's bag for the hospital and transitioned to a closer hotel to the hospital on Nov. 11th in preparation for the scheduled big day. Then we got an unexpected phone call from our attorney. With a sincere apology, she let us know that she had had a long conversation with the surgeon and they were postponing the c-section until Nov. 16th. Oh my! We had not planned to be in Arkansas so long! But apparently the surgeon did not realize when scheduling that our expecting mommy would be only 36 ½ weeks along on November 12th. The surgeon explained that the hospital would be liable for any respiratory distress that could be caused by an intentional premature birth prior to 37 weeks gestation. We had no choice but to wait four more long days, unless it became an emergency situation, which we were not hoping for! Within the final days of waiting, we got an exciting and very timely call from our social worker back in Michigan. Grace's fingerprints had cleared in record time and she was able to complete our home study and was planning to fax it to our attorney's office that day! She explained that she still had other families that had been waiting for their prints for several weeks and even had had theirs submitted prior to Grace's. She seemed quite amazed! We rejoiced in knowing God's favor was with us and He had supplied our need once again.

Finally the day came and we made our way to the family waiting room of the hospital across from the nursery, having made plans to meet our attorney and her husband there. The scheduled time for the baby to be born was rapidly approaching and we were so very excited. Finally the attorney came dressed in full surgical gown, mask, etc. She was to be our birth mom's support person during the delivery. My mind could hardly imagine. No husband, not even a boyfriend, sister, mother, best friend? The reality of her lack of support hit me hard and my heart was filled with compassion. My mind couldn't grasp what felt like a cruel, unfair, injustice that was about to take place. Due to unfortunate circumstances of life, a baby was going to be literally cut out of another woman and placed in my arms for me to love, nurture, cuddle, sing to, and thoroughly enjoy. Desiring to turn her life around, this new mother had made the difficult choice not to parent her child. We rejoiced in knowing that even though abortion could have been an option for her, she chose to give her baby life. Our attorney explained what would be taking place and how she would be back after the baby was born to take us to meet him in the nursery. We excitedly chatted with her husband about adoption, about our growing family, and our Belizean adventure. Soon, a nurse came to escort us to the nursery to meet our newborn son. Thirteen children, seven grandchildren, several nieces, nephews, and I melt at the sight of him; all six pounds and two ounces of him. I watched the nurse as she adjusted the pulse oximeter trying to find a better reading. She had no idea that I was fully aware of the machines and the numbers that weren't looking too good on the screen. Memories flashed through my mind of our granddaughter's first days in NICU and I found myself once again standing beside a baby that was in distress. I watched the monitor and didn't like what I was seeing. In the midst of my mixed emotions of joyful tears and sudden concern for the baby, I heard someone behind me ask, "Is this your first child?" I looked over my shoulder to see a very young, beautiful blond haired woman standing slightly behind us with her crossed arms and a somewhat condescending look all over her face. She introduced herself, "Hi, my name is Lainey; I'm the hospital social worker." After Todd and I told her we had thirteen other children her look became even

more agitated and disapproving. My joy was suddenly stripped and

my tears halted as my mind raced. "If the hospital social worker

doesn't approve of this adoption, is that in any way a threat to us?" I

took a quick inventory in my mind; we have a wonderful supportive

attorney, we have a completed approved home study by a licensed

social worker. We should be good. What damage could her

personal opinion of us possibly do? Suddenly we were asked to

leave the nursery, our baby was in trouble.

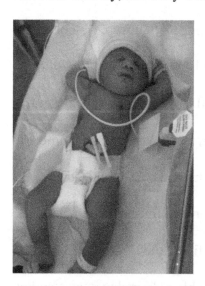

We were aware that there could be possible risks for a baby

born via cesarean section at thirty-seven weeks. I felt prepared and

completely trusted that our new son would overcome his hard

beginning. I soon started feeling convicted and the verse, *"For I am*

not ashamed of the gospel of Jesus Christ......" (Romans 1:16) came

to my mind. I realized that the condemnation I felt for having

fourteen children was in essence the same as being embarrassed for

following the will of God for my life. I had to embrace my identity

in Christ and repent for feeling ashamed of my purpose before I

could walk confidently back into that nursery.

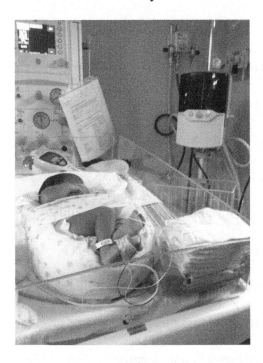

NICU Liam

After several hours, we got the courage to ask what was happening with our baby. They allowed us to go to the Neonatal Intensive Care Unit and see him. The doctor came and explained that they had done x-rays and some other tests that determined that our little one had respiratory distress syndrome. We were told that he could be there for three to ten days, but only time would tell. He was not able to maintain his own temperature, so they had him in a high tech, brand new warming bed. We were not allowed to hold him, feed him or touch him. He had an IV with tubes and wires everywhere. He was receiving 40% of his oxygen by a machine.

As hard as it was to have hardly any contact with him, the cold shoulder we were getting from his nurse made our circumstances all the more uncomfortable. All I could possibly gather from her attitude was that she was not in favor of this adoption. After my first couple of questions, her tone seemed to indicate that we were not exactly welcome there. We looked around at other visiting parents and saw that when they came to visit, chairs were arranged for them to sit next to their babies' isolettes. Not us. For the first two days, we were made to stand while visiting. Our questions were either answered in a way that made us feel less than intelligent, or they weren't answered at all. Returning for

subsequent visits was bittersweet since spending time with our

precious babe meant being terribly uncomfortable in Nurse

Stephanie's presence. We were glad to see the nurses change shifts

when a "new to us", Nurse Melody was assigned to our little guy.

She openly talked to us, answered our questions, and encouraged us.

She was the first one to share how much better the baby seemed to

be doing whenever we were in the room. She was the first one to let

us hold him and feed him as they weaned him off his feeding tube

and encouraged him to drink from a bottle.

The following day my dear, enthusiastic, sensible husband

decided to make the NICU his new mission field. He decided he

was going to do whatever he could to befriend Nurse Stephanie and

find some common ground that would help us connect with her.

Despite her cold shoulder, my husband enthusiastically set about

making small talk about things other than the obvious issues at hand.

Soon he found out that her boyfriend was from Michigan! He really

seemed to make a breakthrough though when he discovered that she

enjoyed and tried to eat all natural healthy foods. He told her about

our bountiful garden harvests every summer and the canning projects the girls and I do. He told her about our family cow and the chickens and pigs we raise on non GMO feed. She seemed impressed that we milked our own cow and made our own butter. Stephanie was communicating with him! Soon we realized that she was beginning to share little things like "Oh, his respirations are up." Soon, we broke through the rough exterior and made a new friend!

Before returning to the hotel late one night, we went to spend some time with our newborn baby and kiss him goodnight. We met his new night nurse, Brandi. Brandi looked into my eyes as if she could see the window of my soul. We connected immediately and I knew she truly cared. She allowed us to take the baby into a small private sitting room for thirty minutes. We could feed him, hold him, and rock him and have some time alone with him. My heart melted as I fell in love with this new precious gift from God and my heart was overflowing with gratitude for the gift of time to be alone with him.

Dad and baby Liam

Since our adoption was considered closed at the request of

his birth mother, we were given a code name for our new son. It was

hospital policy that we were not to refer to him by his name or our

name for confidentiality purposes. So whenever we went to visit,

we would have to pick up the phone that hung on the wall outside of

the NICU door and let them know that "Mickey Mouse's" parents

were there to see him. It sounded dumb and felt even dumber, but if

we wanted them to unlock that door that separated us from our new

baby, we had to conform to the rules no matter how ridiculous they seemed to us. Then one night, Nurse Brandi decided that our son

deserved some dignity. She boldly asked us, "What is his name?"

We were surprised by her interest, so without hesitation we told her,

"His name is William Matthias Weaver and we plan to call him

Liam". I can't accurately explain how good it felt to finally

acknowledge this child as "ours" and he has a real name! It seemed

she also thought it important to give this child the respect he

deserved in calling him by his name. Brandi set about making a

hospital "Record of Birth" certificate complete with his newborn

tiny footprints and our names as Mother and Father "as if" he were

actually born to us and already legally ours!

The next night, Brandi let us know that the whole staff of

NICU nurses was referring to Liam as "Lucky Liam". Pretty soon

the nurses all began teasing us that they were going to climb in our van and go home to Michigan with us too! They said, "There must

be a lot of love at your house!" God had indeed changed their minds

and softened their hearts towards us!

"The King's heart is like a stream of water directed by the Lord;

He guides it wherever He pleases."

Proverbs 21:1

"Lucky Liam" and Nurse Melody (Left)

Morning after morning we made our way from the hotel to

the hospital to visit and spend time bonding with Liam. Then we

would go spend the rest of the day with our girls; 17 year old Livia,

16 year old Raven and 15 year old Jenaya who had traveled with us

and baby Calum, then 8 months old. After tucking Calum in for the

night, we left him with his reliable sisters at the hotel, and headed

back to the hospital to feed Liam and spend some time cuddling him.

One night before we left the hospital, one of the nurses offered us

several cases of formula to take home with us. Liam had been on a

special formula that was quite expensive and these particular cases

were near expiration date so they decided instead of throwing them

away, they would gift them to us. Not only did God put it upon the

nurse's hearts to show us acceptance and kindness but now we were

favored and blessed by the gifts they were sending home with us! It

required a borrowed cart from hospital security to transport all of the

bags of diapers, donated baby quilts and cases of formula to our van!

Getting on and off the elevator day after day we would see

glimpses of Lainey, the Social Worker, in her office. Some days she

managed a smile, but most days we experienced that same look of

disapproval. Nurse Rebecca took over the day shift for Stephanie

about day three of our stay. To our delight, she was very chatty and

friendly. It took no effort on our part to befriend this one! The doctor let us know his progress was slow so he would definitely be in for a full ten days. We were quite concerned as Thanksgiving landed on day ten for Liam and we so desperately wanted to get home to our family. In addition to the stress of dealing with Liam's condition and the treatment of the hospital staff we also were waiting out the five day revocation period which actually turned into seven days since the fifth day fell on a weekend and not on a business day. Like we had learned with Calum in Arkansas, the state allows the birth mother five days in which she can change her mind and decide to parent her child.

At 4:30 pm on Monday, November 23rd, 2016, we watched the clock tick minute after minute as we waited for five o'clock to come; the hour of decision for our birth mother. Time seemed to stand still as we waited the final minutes for that possible dreaded call that so many others have painfully experienced. "Thy Will Be Done Lord", we surrendered time after time as worries and concerns bombarded our minds. Being in a different state, that hospital, with those nurses and that specific baby, was so much more than a coincidence or any plan on our part. This all seemed so much bigger than any desire of our own hearts or any humanitarian effort to "rescue" a fatherless child. It was a divine appointment by a sovereign God in sweet submission and surrender to His will and I am awestruck by His love and compassion towards His people. Of all the other mothers waiting with empty arms, He chose me? It almost seemed unfair. I truly understood Social Worker Lainey's disapproval. It really doesn't make sense from a human perspective. God is in control and He determines the outcomes of our plans and everything we commit to.

Our attorney decided to schedule our court date with the Judge to finalize the adoption the day before Thanksgiving just in case Liam was released and allowed to go home for the holiday. Sure enough, a new doctor on duty decided to sign the discharge papers allowing us to venture home to be with our family just in time for Thanksgiving!

Life with Liam at home was quite a memorable time. Since he had been in the NICU for nine days with respiratory distress, his physician suggested that he stay at home for three weeks to keep him from acquiring any virus that could challenge his immune system and give his lungs more time to recover, develop and become stronger.

From the start, I could tell that Liam was going to require additional and special care.

When I held him, I sensed his stiffness and rigidity. Unlike most newborn infants, he was not floppy, relaxed or trusting. It seemed as if he were possibly exhibiting signs of his birth mother's prenatal stress. He was born addicted to nicotine and that caused him to have slight tremors similar to a drug exposed baby going through withdrawals. He cried a lot for the first four months of his little life in spite of acid reflux medication and trying every possible formula for sensitive tummies on the market. His second mother and big sister Raven, helped me a lot as we took shifts with Liam. I stayed up with him until 4am each day and slept until 8am when I had to get the four of the older children off to the church school where they were attending that year. Raven took the 4am- 8am shift.

Baby Liam

Although Liam was a newborn baby when we came into his life, it was obvious that the rejection he experienced in utero and the abandonment and separation from his birth mother, and her trauma having been incarcerated during her pregnancy had made a profound impact on his developing brain. Liam was nine months old the first time he relaxed in my arms and laid his head on my shoulder. At every baby well check, he amazed us all with the way he was overcoming every obstacle by leaps and bounds! At his eighteen month well check the threat of being referred to a neurologist for further evaluation was no longer a consideration by his physician and we rejoiced over his progress!

Dad & Liam (18 months)

It felt as if we celebrated some sort of seven year jubilee this past summer just prior to celebrating Liam's seventh birthday. We received two very unexpected notices within a few months of one another in the mail. We had had two remaining totally unrelated adoption loans for Liam's adoption. One was from an individual and one from Wee Lambs Adoption Assistance fund. We very unexpectedly received notes in the mail stating that both of our loans were considered paid in full and our debt was canceled and forgiven! Praise The Lord! The total amount owed at that point was just over six thousand dollars. I cried what seemed like buckets of tears of gratitude, praising God for His mercy and loving kindness to us! To this day, I am still in awe of how God orchestrated and made

provision for our ten adoptions. There are no words to describe or

explain it.

William Mathias Weaver – 3 years old

Chapter 10

A Painful Loss - In Memory of Cursten Victoria

"Pride goeth before destruction and a haughty spirit before a fall."

Proverbs 16:18

How does one account for ten successful adoptions and zero failures? A rare feat in the adoption world today to have that many successes and no failures. And if you know anything about adoption, you know that we cannot take credit or blame for the successes or the failures. It is a risky venture that leaves us totally vulnerable and dependent on forces far beyond our control. There are governments, agencies, social workers, consulates, attorneys, birth parents, and lots and lots of red tape to wade through. Surely "adoption is not for the faint at heart". How people get through the process of adoption without the Lord is beyond my comprehension.

Prior to Calum's adoption, I had joined a couple of adoption support groups. My participation in those groups kindled my curiosity to find some understanding in why so many very young couples were having so much trouble adopting, often in addition to the tragic pain of infertility. I noticed that there were many couples that had experienced a lot of failed adoptions. Some as many as thirty times! I tried to reason it out in my mind and questioned, "Why?" Why would God bless me with fourteen healthy, wonderful children while so many were still hoping and praying for just one to fill their empty arms and aching hearts? I felt so unworthy of all these blessings. It started to make sense to me in my own comprehension as I determined that our vision and passion for adoption started with the intention to bring a family to a child in need of a family and not bring a child to a family in need of a child. After Adelyn's adoption, I began to feel adoption was our calling. As God brought more and more children into our family, we started to experience adoption as our personal ministry; taking on the role of missionaries in our own home. I determined that the details, the lessons and the reasons for the blessings are God's business and not mine to figure out.

While having a meal at the table with my family one evening, a very unexpected text came through. It was Calum's birth dad. They were expecting a baby again and they wanted to know if we would adopt the new baby. My mind raced. Who just randomly gets an offer to adopt a newborn baby? After we quickly contemplated the idea, we suggested that maybe we could find someone else to adopt this baby. Then I got another text. "Only you, we want Calum to grow up with his sibling. We won't change our minds." We felt somewhat pressured, but promised them that we would pray. I kept crying out to God with all my heart, it seemed like too much. We would literally just about have triplets. "Thy Will Be Done." We prayed and soon we both felt we couldn't deny the opportunity if this gift was also from the Lord. I felt like a professional as I raced through collecting documents and made copies of our previous SIX home studies for the adoption agency. We only had three months left before the baby was due and she hadn't even seen a doctor yet. We helped Malynna get a prenatal visit set up at a free clinic. Within a few weeks' time we had retained an attorney in Arkansas to handle a private adoption, and

Malynna was soon scheduled for an ultrasound.   With great joy we

found out that we were expecting a baby girl!! Oh how our big girls

rejoiced at the thought of it, after having two little baby boys, a

precious girl would be so much fun! Yet in the midst of the

excitement we knew that there were mountains that would need to be

moved. More than mere obstacles and hurdles, these were big. Two

of our adult children still weren't speaking to us since they became

upset over our last two adoptions and all the negativity that erupted

from those circumstances. We hated to rock their boat once more

and create more waves between us. Our goal and our prayer for the

past two years had been for restoration, forgiveness and

reconciliation. We struggled somewhere between thoughts of

respecting their feelings and not allowing the opinions of other

people dictate and determine our steps.

And then there was the income hurdle. We had exhausted

all our resources and we still owed on adoption loans from Liam's

adoption, but we knew that with God...... even this was possible.

We witnessed the incredible, most powerful hand of God in moving

many mountains before, so in our thinking this was no different.

Our social worker from the agency we had used for the previous two adoptions made it known to us that in her opinion we should not adopt any more children. Our role, she felt, was to mentor others through adoption now. I didn't tell her about all the adoptions I had already mentored over the years and all the matches from Haiti and Liberia that I had already helped facilitate. So we were forced to start all over with a new agency. We prayed and prayed and asked God to lead us, but also prayed sincerely that if this was NOT of Him, we would know enough to lay it all down. Days would go by when I didn't hear from Willow and Malynna and I would get nervous. Then they would call and reassure us, "Oh, we won't change our minds, we want Calum to grow up with his sibling." I had known of others who had done private adoptions but this was all new territory for me.

We arranged for our fingerprinting and police clearances. We filled out applications for a new adoption agency and the additional pages and pages and pages of supporting questionnaires and signatures. We easily fulfilled our 10 hours of required education by attending an annual adoption meeting with over 700 attendees in southern Illinois. Then we hired an attorney in Arkansas to handle the legal requirements for a private adoption. We quickly found out that this private adoption would cost a literal 10% of our last adoption. We counted that as a huge blessing.

Our new attorney was recommended by a friend that was also a member of one of my adoption support groups. Unfortunately, it soon became apparent that this guy wasn't going to be as easily approachable as the last two attorneys we had worked with on domestic adoptions. It required more than one phone call or email correspondence to hear back from him. On an encouraging note, we received a timely unexpected large financial blessing that would more than cover all of our adoption fees.

In the meantime, we struggled with connecting with Calum's birth parents. They shared a cell phone with other family members that lived apart from them so it became rather frustrating. Once again, they were evicted from their apartment during this time and became homeless again. This was the fourth time that we were aware of within a two year time span that they had been evicted and homeless.

The girls and I kept our hearts protected by openly discussing the fact that we were merely walking by faith and we could not just assume that this adoption would work out just because Calum's did. We all immensely enjoyed shopping for newborn baby girl things! We found a beautiful white bassinet and rearranged our bedroom to fit it beside our bed for more soon to be nightly feedings. We found a very nice girly car seat, and all kinds of hair bows, dresses, two piece outfits, onesies, PJs, changing pad for the new baby's dresser that could double as a changing table, crib sheets, and tiny pink and yellow socks complete with tiny little bows on the heels. Homemade newborn crocheted hats in teal green, white and gray complete with matching booties were donated by adoring older sisters that could hardly wait for our little Island princess to appear.

As days became weeks, we bought new and improved proper safety features that would be required to pass the home inspection part of our home study. We bought new baby gates, new fire extinguishers, new stove top knob covers, outlet covers, and new carbon monoxide detectors. It was a requirement that we get our water tested for bacteria and our septic system needed an inspection as well. Todd and I filled out several pages of questionnaires that embarked into some very personal and private areas of our lives.

After what seemed like a long stretch of no communication, I got a text from Willow in Arkansas. Malynna wasn't comfortable working with the attorney we had hired and they wanted us to get a new one. But we had decided that we would not and could not afford to lose what we had invested in the attorney we hired and pay out a new retainer fee on a much more expensive attorney. So we laid it out for them and gave them a choice. They could continue with us and continue with our attorney or they could hire any attorney they wanted, but they would have to find a different family to adopt the baby. It felt like putting all this into their hands was very freeing. We weren't pressing or forcing anything to happen in our favor, but we were hoping they would make a decision and at least let us know what they wanted to do. We attempted to communicate with them in every way possible and never heard from them again. This sweet little family we had embraced as our own with Calum…. maybe we said more than we should have and offended them in a way we did not mean to? Their culture, beliefs and relationships are very different from ours. As hard as it was to lose their trust and lose the possibility of a precious baby girl, I was thankful that Calum was not old enough yet to comprehend what was happening.

Suddenly thoughts came flooding into my mind of what I had all too pridefully shared to some friends and other adoptive parents regarding our perfect adoption record prior to this experience. Ten adoptions, zero fails. I'm not sure what constitutes an adoption failure, but this had to be close. We were in the process and the next thing you know, we weren't. We were expecting a baby, and now we were not.

Off we went back to the consignment shop to resell our baby things. Todd and I had named our sweet unborn princess Cursten Victoria. Cursten meaning, "A follower of Christ". The only logical explanation for the placement, to train her up in the way she should go. It just seemed to fit.

Many months later we finally received word through Calum's maternal grandfather that the baby had passed away in utero. They had lost contact with us when they lost the cell phone they had shared with other family members. We felt some peace and closure in knowing for sure what had happened, although sad for the loss of Calum's baby sister.

Chapter 11

Upstream Pilgrims

"Teach me your way, O LORD, that I may walk in your truth;

unite my heart to fear your name."

Psalm 86:11

Our journey of faith has brought us through many painful

challenges and has led us on a continuum of perpetual spiritual

growth. The narrow way became a whole lot narrower as we

traveled in and out of various denominations, pursuing God and HIS

truth. Swimming against the current of secular society and

mainstream Christianity has been difficult yet rewarding. In spite of all our many twists and turns, God was always there, encouraging us, teaching us, correcting us and guiding us along the way.

Sometime after we had our second daughter, we started attending our former church mainly for the social aspect. This church served us well for a while, but we continued our weekend adventures to our popular neighborhood tavern for the worldly pleasures of drinking and dancing. Soon we stopped attending that church too. Our marriage began to seriously deteriorate as a result of our sinful lifestyle. Todd suggested we find a different church as a last ditch effort to save our dying relationship. A friend of his from work was attending a Church of Christ in a nearby town so we decided to visit there. We attended several months and made great attempts to connect with the people, but it seemed empty and hollow and did not help to fill our spiritual void. We ended up back at the Church of God that previously served our social needs and remained there for many years while our first four children were growing up.

As we became more serious about our relationship with God, we noticed our relationship with each other was growing as well. It was about ten years later when the Lord called us to adopt our daughter Adelyn from Haiti. It was literally a "leap of faith" that sort of rocked our whole church including us.

During our first adoption we experienced a serious lack of support from our church family, so we waited for the Lord to release us as we felt we needed to "go so that we could grow." At this point in our spiritual lives we desired much more than a social club. We have remained friends with some of the families but many of them felt betrayed at our leaving while misunderstanding our motives for adopting. That season was over and we chose to move forward in our pursuit of God.

Our next church experience lasted nine long years. It was while attending this church that the Lord opened the door for us to adopt seven more children; Noah, Raven, Livia and Ian from Haiti and Grace, Jenaya, and Esther from Liberia, West Africa. We had put ourselves under an "anointed" Pastor/ Apostle/ Teacher who had the "gift of prophecy". His wife was his Assistant Pastor and she proclaimed herself to be a "prophetess". We were taught that if we did not have the gift of tongues, we needed to "check our salvation". It was a "health and wealth, name it and claim it" type of church where we applauded loudly when our Pastors entered the sanctuary.

We were expected to give them large amounts of money at a grand Pastor Appreciation Day where elaborately decorated thrones were literally set up for them to sit on during a night of celebration in honor of them. We were taught the evils of never speaking against "God's anointed", so no one dared question anything let alone speak out against anything they said or did.

The Holy Spirit in me grieved and I cringed as antichrist messages were heralded from the pulpit; "If I get cancer and get sick, I will NEVER pray 'Thy will be done,' I will demand my healing!" Such comments came with thunderous laughter, shouting "AMEN!" and applause. He was our "spiritual Father" and we were to go to him with everything and for everything. His charisma, humor and worldly achievements made people respect and trust him. As they would "lay hands" on people, some would fall to the floor supposedly "slain in the spirit", (whatever that means). This church was an African American church and we were the only biracial family. It seemed as if maybe some of the congregation did not appreciate that us "white folks" were raising "black" children. We associated with no one outside of church, but we felt that God had us there for a season and we had to wait for God's timing in releasing us before we could leave. That day came one Sunday morning

during a service when the music was not what our Pastor had

selected and he became very angry, yelling for people to jump to his

commands. In the midst of the drama, I heard a still small voice,

"You shall know them by their fruit." In my mind, the wolf was

being exposed for all to see. We never returned to that church again.

We heard that it was being said that we had demon spirits and that's

why we left.

As we reflected on our experience, it seemed much like a cult

in every sense. In our deception and blindness, if they would have

poured the Kool-Aid we probably would have willingly drunk it,

completely trusting in their leadership. It all sounds so very foolish

to me now, and almost embarrassing to tell, but while in the midst of

deception, we don't ever see how wretched, blind and naked we

really are.

We began to believe at this point that there was some form of

deception in every church and that all churches were apostate. We

looked at the churches we had been in and looked at the world and

there didn't seem to be much difference at all. We continued to pray

fervently for God to show us how to live in the world and not be a part of it. With Jesus alone as our teacher, we daily read our Bibles

for ourselves, searching for truth just like the Bereans.

A couple of years later, after returning from our jungle

adventure in Belize, we had taken another wrong turn in our pursuit

of following after Jesus. Like Christian in Pilgrim's Progress we

suffered and repented for climbing the steep high hill to Mr.

Legality's house. Desperate for some kind of spiritual connection,

we joined this particular church before we fully understood some of

their unique doctrinal teachings and later regretted it. As we studied

our way out of what we came to believe was a false system of belief,

full of deceptions and heresy, we heard the Lord speak to us as

Evangelist spoke to Christian in Pilgrim's Progress:

> *"What dost thou here Christian? Art not thou the man that I*
>
> *heard cry in the City of Destruction? Did not I point out to*
>
> *thee the way to the Wicket Gate? How is it, then that thou*
>
> *has so soon gone out of the way? ..... I pray thee, give more*
>
> *heed to the things that I shall tell thee of. The Lord says,*
>
> *'Strive to go in at the strait gate, the gate to which I send*
>
> *thee, for straight is the gate that leads to life, and few there*
>
> *be that find it. Why didst thou naught the words of God, for*

the sake of Mr. Worldly Wiseman? This is, in truth, the right

name for such as he. The Lord hath told thee that 'he who

will save his life shall lose it.' He to whom thou wast sent for

ease, Legality by name, could not set him free; no man yet

has got rid of his load through him;

He could but show thee the way to woe, for by the deeds of

the law no man can be rid of his load. So that Mr. Worldly

Wiseman and his friend Mr. Legality are false guides; as for

his son Civility, he could not help thee."

(Pilgrim's Progress, John Bunyon, pg. 15- 17)

Through reading Romans, Galatians and Hebrews with fresh

eyes, after much prayer, a good book by Andrew Murray and a great

study on Humility, we recognized that there were some important

aspects and truths missing from that setting. Although painful, we

studied our way out and slowly withdrew from attending the

services. Back we went into holding weekly services and evening

devotions at home with just our family. We researched, read

scripture and examined where we had been. As we considered

where we were going from there, we fasted and prayed for direction for our family. Eventually we accepted our detour as another

valuable learning experience but then it was time to move forward.

We started praying and asking God to show us where were these

people that "call on the name of the Lord with a pure heart?"

(2 Timothy 2:22)

In recalling our time spent in Kentucky with our conservative

brother and sister, we had met on our journey through Mexico from

Belize, we looked online for some kind of a strictly conservative

church in our area that best fit our convictions at the time. The

moderator of a website we had made a request on gave us the name

and address of a church in our area that held similar beliefs. We had

been praying for like-minded believers and we were desperate for

some good fellowship. Somewhat afraid of what we would find

there and thinking it would be a handful of elderly people, we started

desperately seeking out other churches in our area that were

practicing and teaching all that we had come to believe and practice.

With great hope and zeal we visited church after church,

week after week, seeking God with all our hearts. (Jeremiah 29:13)

Finally we gained the courage to visit a conservative Anabaptist

church in a neighboring town. Although we had already forsaken jewelry and make up and trendy immodest clothing, we still stood

out among those wearing extremely conservative uniform attire.

For the first time ever Todd and I sat separately in church. The men

and boys on one side and the women and the girls sat on the other

side. It was excitingly different than I expected. There were more

young than old people! There were many children of every age! I

was in awe of all the young people who had not compromised with

the standards of the world. These people were obviously set apart!

Were these the people we had prayed to find? Here they were

calling on the Lord with a sense of quiet reverence and humility I

had never witnessed. The four part harmony in their acapella

singing of hymns was like music from heaven to my soul. They

looked to the King James Bible alone as their source of truth and

wisdom. We soon learned the governing practices and the biblical

applications of brotherhood assistance, brotherhood accountability,

greeting with a Holy kiss, women's headship veiling, nonresistance,

and the intolerance of divorce and remarriage.

Over time, we struggled with the culture and didn't always

understand its unspoken rules, traditions and language. For the first

two years, we weren't sure where we fit in. I was a fifty four year old mother of adult children, teenage children and two infants under

one year. Instead of fitting into every stage of mothering friends, I

didn't seem to fit into any. It was uncomfortable walking into

church week after week especially for the first several months,

having young children and adults alike stare at me up and down as if

I were something strangely different from themselves even though

we had started dressing exactly the same. In my self- consciousness

I presumed it was my weight, my age, my limp, …. ok, it was "my"

fault that they were so rudely staring at me. But over time I listened

as the little children whispered comments to each other about other

"worldly, wicked" people walking by. My Lord! My heart grieved.

Had not these children learned to love and respect the souls of

people rather than simply judging them as wicked and evil people

based on their external appearance?

In that culture it seemed acceptable to frequently make sure

our adopted children knew they were "different" and this was painful

for all of us. Remarks about the color of their skin or the texture of

their hair were often innocently and ignorantly made by adults and

children alike. Some people within our conservative circle were

very curious about what it is like for us having "come out of the world". They wondered what we saw in them from an unbiased viewpoint having not grown up in conservative Christian home.

To be honest, I always felt as if I was on the outside looking in. They possessed something I will never have, like the innocence of my Amish sister I admired on our trip through Mexico. I knew there would always be cultural cues, language differences and unwritten rules that would continue to be strange to me because I didn't grow up learning these things by example. It seemed as if their zeal to acknowledge their own modest, outward apparel as a reflection of the inner condition of their hearts spilled over into condescending looks towards others that didn't quite share those same convictions. I was once on the other side of that fence! I too am one of those wicked, evil sinners that Jesus came to die for but it has very little to do with the way I am outwardly dressed.

"Man looks at the outward appearance but God looks at the heart."

1 Samuel 16:7

The true gospel came to life for me as I read and reread the gospels, and the Bible as a whole. I finally met the real Jesus, the

Bread of Heaven and the Living Water as I set about the task of

fasting and praying for freedom from deceptions and repenting with

Godly sorrow for the sins that had ensnared me throughout my life.

All through my Christian journey in and out of several churches and

denominations, I never was exposed to the real Jesus that had the

power to set the captives free. I had never witnessed deliverance

from sin, true humility, and brotherly love in action all at once.

Throughout our 40 years of wandering through the

wilderness, we have learned and experienced a lot. In our pursuit of

the narrow way, God taught us something about Himself and our

relationship to Him through every turn. Thankfully, He was still in

control even when we went astray. Our twists and turns in our

journey have always been opportunities for God to teach and

discipline us. I came to appreciate every lesson learned from every

religious setting we had experienced, although I have sort of been

somewhat envious of people with denominational roots to raise their

children in. Unfortunately we have not successfully kept the hearts

of our children for Jesus as they became weary in all of our

wandering and chose to make their own way in this world. Our prayer is that they too will find their way back to the Lord and choose to surrender their lives to Him.

We are currently two years into probably one of the healthiest church environments we have ever been in where Jesus is truly the head of the body. We had left our previous setting with strong concerns over their lack of zeal for reaching the lost and willingness to make disciples. We felt as if we had found where God would have us when we walked into our present church hearing every service start with this announcement; "We are here to make disciples". We have successfully held onto some of our conservative convictions and beliefs while worshiping in this not so extremely conservative setting. We are learning, but more importantly, unlearning some not so helpful doctrines of men taught through some of our former church settings. We don't know for sure what the future holds for us, but we do know who holds our future. Through our journey and especially now I have come to realize the truth in that there are no perfect churches because there are no perfect people. Our pilgrimage continues as we strive to open our hearts, our minds and our lives to all the Lord has for us.

Chapter 12

The Blessing of Oppression and Trials

"Satan comes to steal, kill and destroy,

but I come that you may have life more abundantly."

John 10:10

It seemed the oppression we experienced in the beginning of our adoption journeys was due to differences in skin color, then it became more about our number of children, then it became more about our advancing age. It seems we have experienced a lot of different forms of opposition from the very beginning in some form or another.

Recently I attended a birthday party with my two youngest sons. The conversation was started by a middle aged woman who was babysitting two young boys for a friend for the weekend. Her comments quickly displayed her disapproval of her friend's decision to adopt the extremely active young boys out of foster care as a single mom, especially at "her age". "There's a reason women quit

giving birth after forty," she freely shared. My heart sank. "Here we

go again", I thought to myself. I had no words to offer. I had just

celebrated my 60th birthday and here I was observing my six and

seven year old sons playing with the other children at the party. I'm

sure I had already been labeled the grandmother by the younger

mom's chatting around me. I decided not to comment. It seemed as

if she probably wouldn't understand if I explained to her that just

maybe, her friend's decision to adopt at her age wasn't ever really

about her at all. Maybe, she saw a need and decided to fill it,

believing she could do it, even though she was beyond child bearing

years. When I hear these naysayers, I wonder about Sarah and

Elizabeth. I can only imagine the comments and the opposition they

may encounter these days in spite of what most people with a

Biblical worldview would consider God ordained miracles. Surely a

precious gift from God cannot be undermined by misunderstandings

and comments by those who may have misinterpreted what God has

been doing in and for us and our children.

At the conception of Adelyn's adoption in 1996, our oldest

biological daughter had some serious reservations about us adopting.

I knew that if we would have collaborated with her prior to conceiving her other three younger biological siblings, she would have had a lot to say about that as well. My very best friend encouraged me to respect our teenage daughter's feelings and let go of this crazy idea of adopting another child, but I knew without a doubt this was a movement of God and I felt more than a strong pull to walk into it at all costs. One day, prior to following through with our first appointment with our adoption agency's social worker, I felt miserably torn between following what I believed was God's will, and respecting our oldest daughter's opinion and feelings. I decided to fast and pray for a day which wasn't something I was used to practicing at that time. As evening came, I cried out to God and asked Him to please speak to me. In my spiritual immaturity, just like we've always been warned and told NOT to do, I opened my Bible and started reading where it fell open, expecting God to speak to me. Tears ran down my cheeks and peace, incredible peace flooded my soul as I read a message from God's word I had never seen before:

"Don't trust anyone, not your best friend or even your wife;
For the son despises his father and the daughter defies her mother.

> *The daughter-in-law defies her mother-in-law.*
> *Your enemies are right in your own household!"*
>   Micah 7: 5-6

I've come to understand, since then, that we should not expect people to understand our calling, and as mature adults, we are entitled to make our own decisions despite the differing opinions and perspectives of others no matter how good their intentions may be. Never could I have imagined that a seemingly "good" thing to do could cause and create such opposition from other people who would claim to understand God's will for our lives better than us. As a persecuted Brother from China, Brother Yun clearly expresses this in his book, "Living Water";

> *"When God reveals His plans and strategies to us, we must move forward in obedience and be willing to withstand attacks and opposition. We need to recognize that just because a heavenly calling has come to our lives; it doesn't mean everything will go smoothly. In fact, it could be argued that Satan only attacks those plans that he knows originates from God's throne. Other kinds of plans and programs that Christians are involved with are little threat to Satan's*

kingdom on this earth. But when our adversary senses something has God's anointing on it, he is afraid, for such strategies can blow his evil kingdom to pieces. The disciples of Jesus received a calling from God to take the gospel to the ends of the earth. They went forth in obedience and in the power of God, and they paid a dear price for their service."

(Living Water, Brother Yun, pg. 42)

We have had our share of critics. We have been ostracized by many of our own brothers and sisters in Christ for following the will of God for our family. Prior to the conception of our first adoption, I came to understand that God is looking for willing servants, not necessarily perfect people. I trusted that to be true, fully aware of my own faults, failures, insecurities and inabilities. Like all my fellow believers, I too am just a sinner, saved by God's amazing grace, in need of a sinless Savior with a willingness to allow Him to progressively transform me into His likeness. I have not done anything "perfectly" and I have been far from what I or anyone would consider a perfect child, wife, mother or friend. I've made more than my share of mistakes. I am fully aware of this, but I find comfort in knowing that God in His sovereignty knew all of that in advance. He knew I was not going to perfectly measure up to the task, yet despite my human failures, He has been faithful to me and to my family and forever I will be grateful.

We had been living under some serious scrutiny and oppression as many family members opposed our Christian walk and our God given purpose. Our oldest children were strongly influenced by some family members that seriously believed that our biological children's lives would have somehow been better off had we not adopted additional children. Once, a close relative caught wind that we had run out of propane gas in the middle of a cold February day. Instead of kindly checking in with us to see if we were okay or if we needed a warm place for the children to stay, a call was made to child protective services out of "concern for the children". By the time my husband got home from work that afternoon, our son Chad had already helped to resolve the problem and we had heat once again. Then at 10 pm that night, while getting ready for bed, we heard a knock on our front door. A police officer and a social worker stepped into our house and let us know that they had received a call. "Mam, I'm sorry to bother you, it's obvious you have heat, but we received a complaint that there were many children living here without heat." As the social worker's eyes scanned the rooms she could see from the door, the police officer apologized for the inconvenience. I explained the situation and how it had been resolved earlier that day. They left without incident but we were left feeling vulnerable and confused that our own family would do this to us without considering the severity of the consequences to the children they were intending to help. It seemed by the way the situation was handled that the call was not made out of any real compassion or sincere concern for our children since they didn't seem to have any desire to have a relationship with the ones they were attempting to rescue or protect. It seemed more like a hateful vengeance that was bent on hurting us without considering or caring about the damage that could have been done had their plan succeeded. Twelve years later, we would find out who had exactly made that call and she confessed. She also shared who was involved in encouraging that decision. Surprisingly, the anger and resentment was all gone, and I had no room in my heart for ill feelings toward her at all. "Father, forgive them for they know not what they do."

Rude comments, misunderstandings, different perspectives and strong opinions against our calling couldn't even begin to compare with the opposition yet to come.

One dreary late September day, I was sitting in our dining room filling out an application for a family membership at our local YMCA when I heard a knock on our front door. To my shock it was Child Protective Services (again). Having been previously educated by fellow home schoolers and adoptive parents with big families with children from difficult places who had traveled down this same road before, I knew enough not to answer any questions and not to allow the social worker entrance to our home without a warrant from a Judge.

At every question, I did my best to only affirm that I would prefer to wait until my husband was home to answer any questions, which also bought us time to speak with an attorney. I was told that he needed to see all the children in the house within 48 hours of his first visit, so we made arrangements for him to return on Friday since Todd would be home from work then. Just before he left, he said, "I want you to know that ninety percent of complaints are bogus." My mind raced. Just the possibility of having my children taken from me was more than a horrifying thought, for them and for me. My accusers surely knew that taking my children from me would be like ripping my heart out of my chest. I wasn't too concerned about Esther and Ian. Even though they were minors, they had a voice of their own and could speak for themselves; but my little innocent two and three year old boys whom we had had since birth, who only knew us as their only parents and caregivers.... and my sweet Calum who shied away from strangers and had never been left with any babysitter other than a loving, trusted older sister. They were incapable of communicating on their own behalf.

> *"When we come under such an attack, we need to know who*
> *we are in Christ, and we need to know the one we are*
> *serving. We must focus our eyes on the goal to which God*
> *has called us and not allow the attacks of the enemy to take*
> *us off the path on which we are called to walk."*
> (Living Water, Brother Yun, page 274)

I hung onto his parting words. Why did he tell me that? Ninety percent of all complaints are bogus? Wow. I had no idea

what the complaint against us was, but I surely did know who was
vengeful, angry and bitter within our family, so the "who" part of the
equation wasn't hard to figure out. As a somewhat proactive person,
I started making phone calls; first to our Pastor, asking for prayer.
Then I called our family doctor and made emergency appointments
for our little boys. I told her what was going on and she graciously
did immediate physical assessments on each of the boys and
attempted numerous calls to CPS to speak to the social worker on
our behalf. She had been seeing the boys for all their scheduled
well checks on a routine basis since they were newborn babies and
from her professional opinion, she had absolutely no concerns about
the boys being neglected or abused and she was quite willing to
advocate on our behalf. Interestingly, one of the allegations we
would soon find out was that we didn't believe in doctors and that
our children did not receive adequate medical care. Her professional
opinion and documentation proved otherwise.

Before Todd even returned from work that day, I quickly
contacted Home School Legal Defense and spoke with an attorney
who would help us and walk us through the investigation and defend
us in court if necessary. We had been members and supporters of

this organization for several years but I had hoped to never need their services. Actually, we were able to quickly dismiss home schooling as an issue since Esther and Ian were both over sixteen years old and legally old enough to choose not to attend public school in the state of Michigan and at two and three years old, Calum and Liam weren't of school age yet. We were advised to write down whatever the allegation(s) were so we could report back to them. We were warned not to give any information, defend ourselves, or react in any way to the complaints.

Friday came and we made sure all the children were home so they could be seen by the social worker. There were seven living at home then, although Grace was attending a six week mission training school in New York City. The first items discussed were the ages and birthdates of the children. It seemed unavoidable not to share this important information, and it didn't feel threatening at all to do so. To our advantage, the family member who made the allegations didn't even know the correct ages or number of children in the home. To his surprise, the majority of the complaints were pretty much concerns about adult children who were no longer living at home and were not minors so CPS really had little reason to be involved, but to our benefit, he followed through with the investigation anyways.

In keeping with the instructions we were given by our attorney through Home School Legal Defense, I uncomfortably yet emotionlessly sat stone faced through the reading of the extremely difficult to hear allegations with the CPS Social worker without responding to any of it.   I had always struggled with understanding how Jesus never tried to defend himself when He was accused;

"Pilate asked Jesus, 'Are you king of the Jews'?

Jesus replied, 'You have said it'.

Then the leading priests kept accusing him of many crimes,

and Pilate asked him,

'Aren't you going to answer them?

What about all these charges against you?'

But Jesus said nothing, much to Pilate's surprise."

Mark 15: 2-5

I patiently wrote down every allegation as he read off twenty six complaints that had been made against us. TWENTY SIX? That alone gave me some insight as to why he might suggest that we may be in that ninety percent bogus complaint category. It sounded to me as if someone was trying as hard as possible to bury us alive and come up with any and every possible story that could potentially warrant the removal of our minor children.

The following day, I openly sobbed when I called our attorney to read the long list of disturbing allegations to him over the phone. I repeatedly tried to regain my composure as I read through the disturbing list of twenty six complaints. When I finally made it through, he paused and calmly said to me:

"Blessed are ye when men shall revile you and persecute you and shall say all manner of evil against you falsely ....."

Matthew 5:11

I surely wasn't feeling blessed at the time. I was feeling betrayed by people I dearly loved and in danger of losing the most precious things in my life. I didn't even know this person I was speaking to over the phone, but I knew he was experienced in these situations and possessed a much greater wisdom than my own. I trusted him as we visited each and every allegation and spent time reflecting on the truths, the half-truths and the whole blatant lies. In acknowledging the first complaint on the list was that I was mentally

ill, the attorney went on to say that it sounded more like the one who

came up with these allegations was the one who actually was

mentally ill. He not only possessed great wisdom, but now I knew

he also had great discernment.

"In this world you will have trouble, but take heart!

I have overcome the world."

John 16: 33

We had set up an appointment for the social worker to return

to do interviews with each family member. Friday afternoon came,

we had been fasting and praying for three consecutive days and had

a collection of documentation and lists of references, both

professional and character witnesses who had been involved in our

lives over the past several decades. Our Pastor and his wife came to

spend the day in support of Todd and me and our dear children. He

was very helpful and able to speak to the lack of credibility in a few

of the statements that were made about us and our "spiritual

instability". Thankfully, that particular denomination has a system of checking up on the church backgrounds and history of seeking

members to prevent potential issues that need to be resolved from

being spread from church to church. Having that type of

professional advocate proved to be extremely valuable in defending

our integrity.

Over the course of the afternoon, six of us took turns

privately being interviewed by the social worker. He decided it was

not necessary to interview our two little boys after he realized that

they would not cooperate with him alone without us in the room.

We had been forewarned at how the simplest of well-meaning

statements could easily be twisted or misconstrued, so our attorney

made the suggestion that we keep our answers short and to the point.

I felt a peaceful presence in the midst of an extremely stressful

situation when it was my turn for what felt like an interrogation. I

had to sign some paperwork before the questions began. "How many

dogs do you have?" "Five." I answered. "Did you move to Belize

because you thought the world was ending?" he asked. "Isn't Belize

part of the world?" I asked. He smiled. "Are you mentally ill?" he

asked. "I don't think so. I've never been told I should get help by

family or friends or my doctor or my counselor or anyone significant in my life. We've passed several adoption home studies through

three different agencies and I've had three voluntary psychological

evaluations for Haitian adoption requirements. In order to adopt

from Haiti, you have to have a psychological evaluation by a

licensed psychologist," I explained. I was armed with strong

professional documentation, evidence that proved my accuser's mere

opinions of me to be false:

> PAGE 4
> Noreen Weaver
> Psychological Testing Report
>
> FORMULATION AND CONCLUSIONS:
>
> Ms. Weaver was self-referred for the purposes of a
>
> psychological evaluation. She and her husband are currently
>
> seeking the adoption of a Haitian infant and it is
>
> recommended that they complete a psychological evaluation
>
> for the adoption process.
>
> Psychological evaluation results suggest that Ms.
>
> Weaver is absent of any significant emotional, psychological
>
> or personality disorder that would impair her ability to
>
> function in the community, at home, or at work. Mental
>
> Status Examination reveals no significant impairment in

memory, intellectual functioning, judgment, thought process, mood or behavior.

RECOMMENDATIONS:

Due to the data gathered in the psychological evaluation, it appears that there are not any psychological or emotional disorders that would significantly interfere with this client's ability to parent.

Randy Fxxxx, M.A., L.L.P, Michigan License #8xxx

In addition to the psychological evaluations, I offered to show the social worker our home studies and updates we had accumulated over the years. I assumed the most relevant was the most recent home study report since I was fairly confident that one of the two adult children who had opposed Calum's adoption obviously had a lot to do with initiating this investigation. Their interview remarks with our social worker had been reported and were written in our home study, so their reasons for opposing our most recent adoptions were well documented. I could see past the faces of the ones I so dearly loved and could see the adversary at work, attempting to disrupt what God had ordained.

"Our battles are not against flesh

but against principalities and powers in heavenly places...."

Ephesians 6:12

I gave the social worker our family doctor's name and phone number and informed him that she had been trying to connect with him by phone to advocate on our behalf. I gave him a long list of personal and professional references complete with contact information.

After the interviews concluded, he needed to see the rest of our home and the bedrooms where all of our children slept. We took our time in showing him that all bedroom doors lock only from the inside, so no one was being locked in their rooms. Two of our bedrooms had access to a private bathroom, so no; children were not being locked in their rooms without access to a bathroom. All children were visually at a normal weight or above, so no, no one was being locked in their room being deprived of food. We enjoyed giving him a tour of our full walk out basement where apparently we were said to be operating a puppy mill. To his amazement, most of the basement walls were neatly lined with many shelves of home

canned green beans, kidney beans, black beans, pinto beans, stewed

tomatoes, tomato juice, potatoes, carrots, venison, chicken, corn,

applesauce and strawberry preserves. In the center of the main room

there was a small blue kiddie pool with our daughter Raven's

Australian Shepherd, Kassie and her THREE newborn puppies.

From what he had been told, he said he expected to see rows of dog

crates stacked one on top of the other. Yes, we raise puppies, but no,

we are not a puppy mill. Although we were accused of not believing

in higher education and not allowing our children to pursue their

personal career choices, Grace was at a mission school in New York

at the time and myself, Addie and Grace were currently enrolling

and had been accepted to Liberty University for online studies.

Ironically, my pursuit was to pursue a degree in social work. I had

already accumulated 60 college credits as a nursing student several

years prior. Although the twenty six allegations were nothing more

than vicious lies and twisted half-truths, the one completely true

accusation stood out to us among all the rest.

He never questioned us about or mentioned the complaint that we "pretend to home school our children" or the particular one truth that stood out to us; "They tell their children God will not hear their prayers if they are disobedient." Although the Bible speaks to this truth, we determined by this that our persecutor was either not a Christian or just obviously very ignorant of this scriptural truth.

"If one turns his ear from hearing God's law,

even his prayer is an abomination."

Proverbs 28:9

"Now we know that God does not hear sinners;

but if anyone is a worshiper of God

and does his will, He hears him."

John 9:31

"If I had harbored sin in my heart,

the sovereign Master would not have listened.

If I regard wickedness in my heart,

the Lord will not hear."

Psalm 66:18

Thankfully, in God's loving kindness and mercy, He blessed

us with a Christian social worker who was also a neighbor we had

not yet met, and a home schooling father of three children! I had

met and spoke with his wife a couple of times and she had told me

her husband worked for Child Protective Services. In retrospect, I

believe those to be providential meetings.

Our church family agreed to fast and pray with us for three

days prior to the interviews. Out of desperation, my prayer became

one of complete and total surrender. "Father, you gave these

children to me. If I am the monster that they are saying I am, if I am

guilty of all these terrible things, if I am deceived and my

perspective of myself is not in keeping with what is actually true of

me, if I am guilty of these heinous activities, then I pray that you

would take these children from me and find me guilty. If in your

wisdom, You determine that I don't deserve to have them, let them

be taken away." I honestly felt serenity and peace in praying "Thy

will be done." I felt content in knowing and trusting and believing

our adversary would not win this one, no matter what the outcome might look like based on human perspectives. I would join God and

stand with Him and trust that whatever happened, I would submit to

His will no matter what, just as I had when God gave them to me.

For the first days and weeks into the investigation, I had only

thought of my own personal pain and the terror the boys would go

through if forced to be torn from their family and all things safe,

secure and comfortable in their little world. But through some

supernatural shift, I was able to rise above my feelings and that of

my precious babies and pray on a whole new level without emotion.

RC Sprouls once said, "If you know God, you want him to dominate

your thinking."

After all interviews were complete, Todd ushered the social

worker to our front door. Oblivious to the reason for this strange

man's reason for coming to our home, our confident and boisterous

two year old Liam reached out to shake our visitor's hand. "I don't

see anything here that concerns me," he said with a big grin as he

turned to walk out our front door.

"God's way is perfect. All the Lord's promises are true.
He is a shield to all who look to Him for protection."

Psalm 18:30

It was over. In our seemingly helpless, darkest time of trouble, our faith was tested. The victory was bittersweet as we still had to emotionally deal with the fact that we had been betrayed by people we deeply loved, had given much of our lives to and cared so very much about.

"It is not an enemy that taunts me - I could bear that.

It is not my foes who so arrogantly insult me –

I could have hidden from them.

Instead, it is you- my equal, my companion and close friend.

What good fellowship we once enjoyed

as we walked together to the house of the Lord....

But I will call on God and the Lord will rescue me....

I will cry out in my distress and the Lord hears my voice.

He ransoms me and keeps me safe from the battle waged against me,

Though many still oppose me."

Psalm 55: 12-18

After the investigation was closed, since it seemed there was a pattern of false reports by family members, we were told that if we were reported again that they would be told that we have already been investigated. Vengeance, hatred and anger are sinister. No wonder Jesus likened anger to murder. It's very dangerous and destructive. Satan comes to kill, steal, and destroy. He truly hates marriage, adoption, the family unit, and every other institution God created. Sin separates, love unites.

We received a copy of the investigation report after several weeks of waiting for that specific confirmation that the investigation was actually closed. It was extremely difficult to read. Not only was a call made by a close family member who had been estranged since Calums adoption, but a lengthy email as well, describing several stories; some completely fabricated, some strongly exaggerated, and some explaining examples of parenting failures and personal mistakes spanning thirty plus years. The report also revealed that CPS had tried to get the police involved and they refused citing no criminal activity had taken place.

I was especially pleased to read in the detailed report that our "housekeeping standards were above normal" despite the accusation of having a puppy mill in our basement. It was somewhat sad but amusing to me how my girls and I had frequently, freely and lovingly traveled sixty four miles round trip to clean the home of the ones who made that call to Child Protective services. I will forever keep the seven page Child Protective Services investigation report as it is a symbol to me of how God intervenes on behalf of his children and how justice always prevails when we seek first the Kingdom of God and HIS righteousness.

Some of our children have come from some seriously hard places and they struggle with being honest in their communications due to trust and attachment issues. We've always told them that we can't hide the truth; truth will always come to the light. Two years later, after the CPS trauma, I got a surprise phone call on Mother's Day from an estranged daughter who confessed and apologized for taking part in instigating the latest investigation. She said she was angry at the time. We found out, through the actual report, who had turned us in and it wasn't her, but she was not shy about sharing who was involved. Her bitter stories were a catalyst and basis for many of the allegations against us. It wasn't difficult to show her mercy and forgiveness. I acknowledged that I, too, needed her forgiveness as well for my part in not handling some things well that had led to

her becoming angry.

"Truthful words stand the test of time, but lies are soon exposed."
Proverbs 12:19

Although I know that what was done to us was malicious,

devious and destructive, I also understand that what my accusers

meant for evil, God has used for good. (Genesis 50:20) I never

imagined that anything so painful would become a blessing and

could change the trajectory of my life. My betrayers may never

know how much they have helped me to become more like Jesus in

my suffering. I had always cared too much about what other people

thought and said about me, confusing Satan's lies with God's truth. I

was truly a people pleaser and I denied my own identity for the sake

of people who did not really care about me or truly have God's best

interest at heart. I have come to understand the error of my own

ways and taken responsibility for my wrongs making apologies

where I felt it was necessary. I have learned a great deal about

myself and the peace and strength God is able to provide during painful circumstances. I have experienced God's forgiveness and mercy over and over again, and I've learned that my identity is secure in Jesus Christ alone and not in the perspectives and opinions of others.

"No weapon formed against you shall ever prosper,

and every tongue which rises against you in judgment

you shall condemn.

This is the heritage of the servants of the Lord,

and their righteousness is from me, says the LORD."

Isaiah 54:1

Chapter 13

Healing By His Grace

"We demolish arguments and every pretension that sets itself up

against the knowledge of God,

and we take every thought captive

and make it obedient to Christ."

2 Corinthians 10:5

The depth of my healing took a whole new course after the

brokenness of a betrayal left me reeling for answers to a myriad of

questions. I was at the end of myself. I knew I had to seriously

challenge and modify my own beliefs and dig to discover whatever

my responsibility was is all of this. My perspectives of myself, God and others were not exactly consistent with truth. I knew my Lord had no intentions for me to retaliate or respond in any negative way to our experience. I fully understood that vengeance belongs to God. It was not an option nor was it in my heart to hurt them back in return. I chose to pray for those who had intentionally hurt us. If it's true that hurting people hurt people, then these people were obviously hurting, therefore my response or lack of response would need to come from a heart of compassion. I began to comprehend how hurting people tend to interpret every action through the lens of their own pain and how our past pain often spills into our present. I recognized that my unresolved pain was causing other people pain so I had to do the work it required to get help for myself, knowing the only one I could "fix" now was myself by the grace of God. I have since learned that we are not capable or responsible for fixing other people, yet we can be influential in helping others heal by being willing to grow in our own self-reflection and learn to manage and regulate our own emotions in a mature and respectful manner. It became obvious to me that we cannot guide anyone beyond a stage of character development that we ourselves have not already attained.

Throughout many years of trials, the Word of God became increasingly more and more precious to me. I determined to memorize larger passages of scripture. Psalm 19 became one of my favorite chapters and helped me to get my focus off myself and onto my Creator. Throughout all creation, God has witnessed His love for us. Even the heavens declare His glory. What if our love for God is only evident to the world by the way we treat the people around us? Love is the one thing we were commanded to do. "Love one another…" John 15: 34

It's true that we gravitate to what we focus on so I wanted to immerse myself in the Lord's thoughts. I knew I could choose growth, healing and restoration in humility or I could stay stuck in unforgiveness and bitterness in my pride. I gained a new appreciation for the virtue of humility in taking responsibility for and recognizing my own weaknesses, imperfections, character flaws, mistakes and sins. My pride, arrogance and hypocrisy usually had taken the form of defensiveness, or unwillingness to own any responsibility for my own wrongs while blaming others for theirs. In humility I consider others better than myself, in my pride I view myself better than others. I knew in my heart that I would only be hindering my own walk with Christ if I didn't walk in humility and

work toward extending love and forgiveness.

"Fools think their own way is right but the wise listen to others."

Proverbs 12:19

I began evaluating my own many self-defiling mental

attitudes such as worry, fear and self-pity. I knew if I didn't

properly process what had happened to us and if I didn't do it God's

way, I would remain bitter, resentful and stuck in my negative

pattern of thinking. If we do nothing, nothing changes, and I knew

that something had to change! It became a genuine desire of my

heart to deal with my circumstances and my relationships in a

mature, respectful and responsible manner that would bring healing

for myself and possibly others while honoring my Lord. I was more

than willing to take responsibility for whatever was my fault and

own it so that I could also intentionally let go of what was not mine

to carry. Creating boundaries to protect my own heart also became

necessary. My real challenge came in distinguishing between my

reality and the deceptions of the enemy. The lines between Satan's hateful lies and God's loving truths seemed indistinguishable before

I started taking a deeper, more focused look at what God had to say.

By bringing up the sins of my past, my adversary wanted me to

believe I was unworthy of redemption or forgiveness. Yet my

Savior said He would clothe me in His righteousness. My adversary

wanted me to be punished without mercy. Yet my Savior said

goodness and mercy would follow me all the days of my life. My

adversary wanted me to feel worthless. My Savior said I was bought

with the price of his blood. I began learning to combat the lies with

truth.

I have worked very hard to overcome many lies and limiting

beliefs the adversary had planted and formed in my mind over the

years. I came to the realization that Jesus came for broken fallen

humanity and that included me too! To be extended such wondrous

grace from God strongly suggested to me that we are to show

abundant grace to others in return. Changing the way I saw things

became a new opportunity I had never appreciated before. I had to

learn to see past myself and my feelings whether valid or not and

accept that my interpretation of things isn't the only perspective. My

perspectives have been shallow and unfortunately my actions have not always lined up with my beliefs. Thankfully a person is more

than the sum of his or her mistakes. Jesus came for the sick and the

broken. I would claim to be one of those people. I am learning from

my mistakes, but my righteousness is in Jesus and not in my own

works. I began to understand that if I desired and accepted God's

grace for my imperfect self, I needed to be sure to extend that same

level of grace to other imperfect people as well.

"For all have sinned and fall short of the glory of God."

Romans 8:23

Although we had determined to "do better" than our parents,

we had never strongly considered that we learn to parent from our

parents. So what was "normal" for us growing up was not Christ-

like behavior. Being an approval seeker, being frightened of angry

people, stuffing my feelings, being fearful of abandonment and

judging myself and others harshly were all characteristics of living

with and being raised by emotionally sick people. Unknowingly, the

effects had trickled down from us to our oldest children. I had never

really made the connection or blamed my parents for my issues or for who I had become. I always believed that my problems and my

need for growth and change were my responsibility not someone

else's fault. Tony A., who invented and wrote the Laundry List of

fourteen traits of an adult child of alcoholic/ dysfunctional families

wrote this;

"Alcoholism is a family disease; we became para alcoholics and took

on the characteristics of that disease even though we didn't pick up

the drink."

(Adult Children Of Alcoholics, pg. 10-11)

       I could see a reflection of myself in many of those fourteen

traits. I honestly did not realize that I was affected beyond what I

already knew to be true of me and I certainly had no idea that the

influence of an alcoholic parent had ingrained strong residual effects

well beyond childhood. I had a lot of healing to do without realizing

it. I had to work to acknowledge the emotional wounds from my

past. Although I understood there were enduring effects of being an

ACA (Adult Child of an Alcoholic), I struggled with the notion that

this list of traits could be labeled as a "disease". Was I a "victim" of

this "disease" or responsible for the ongoing dysfunction it caused?

Or both? I was well aware that our parents must have also

experienced some level of dysfunction in their childhoods.

Dysfunction has a deep generational root, but instead of playing

victim in a perpetual never ending blame game, it seemed more

appropriate and productive to deal with my own present state. I

could either grow from my experiences or be crushed by them.

Taking the victim role and blaming my parents for their emotional

immaturity, lack of spiritual guidance and their poor choices in life

has never occurred to me. I absolutely believe my parents did the

best parenting job they were capable of doing at the time. I hold no

resentments against them and if I still had the opportunity I would

definitely be much more intentional about honoring them simply

because God commands it whether I deemed them "worthy" or not.

"No amount of regret changes the past.
No amount of anxiety changes the future.
But any amount of gratitude changes the present."
(Marc & Angel Chernoff)

I discovered that we were not alone in our painful loss of

adult child relationships. All over the world, adult children are

estranging from their parents at an alarming rate. In the days we are living in, it seems to be a common practice to disown and alienate a family member for various reasons. In 2020, research done by a sociologist named Karl Pillemar showed that 1 in 4 Americans are estranged from their families. Fostering strong relationships through compassion requires a willingness to see life through the eyes of another person.   If we are to exemplify Jesus Christ, we are called to love and care for others, not disown them or condemn them by our judgements.   I've heard it said that avoiding conflict IS conflict.

"People may be right in their own eyes

but the Lord examines their heart."

Proverbs 21: 2

When I took a cognitive behavior therapy practitioner course to help myself interpret the source of my own issues, it seemed the instructor frequently quoted analogies from the Bible. He did not give credit to the obvious source yet claimed not to have any religious affiliation or system of belief. I realized then how the answers we seek literally are already there for us in God's word and even secular psychologists are picking up on God's wisdom and selling it for a price. There is literally nothing new under the sun, we just need to seek and apply the wisdom God has already given us.

I have discovered that self-esteem is a choice. I realize now that self-esteem is not nearly as important as God esteem. No one else can control how I feel about myself and it has been my privilege to investigate and discover God's thoughts towards me. Actually, while agonizing and looking within myself for value, I was unknowingly practicing idolatry. I was looking within myself for self-worth when the One I needed to look to was Jesus and to HIS worth. Corrie Ten Boom said it best: "Look within, be depressed. Look around, be distressed. Look to Jesus, be at rest."

I could choose to live with the label and blame other people for my lack of esteem, or I could choose to reframe my thoughts and choose to believe something very different.

Personal growth has required me to obtain the ability to see from God's frame of reference. My interpretations haven't always been accurate. No one has a truly subjective perspective. We are all limited by what we can see. For example, we are blessed to have all four complete gospels. Four similar, yet different accounts of the life and influence of our Redeemer written by four men based on their perspectives and experiences in their relationship to Jesus, his life and ministry. Matthew, Mark, Luke and John each wrote from a different perspective. They each witnessed the same accounts only from different angles and we can respect those differences knowing all of their messages are inspired by God.

I could choose to go through life staring in the rear view mirror, blaming other people for my problems instead of taking responsibility and recognizing the present in front of me and future ahead of me. While choosing to stay stuck in my negative, irresponsible and immature thinking there was a tendency to only remember all the bad things other people have said and done and forget all the bad things that I have said and done. In my prideful state, these deletions in memory were quite convenient but not helpful at all. Holding onto the pain of my past was taking away from the vision of what was before me. I cannot change what has happened to me in my past, but I can change the impact the past has on me. It is possible to resolve issues from the past in order to be free of anger, hurt, unforgiveness, bitterness and resentments. Inaccurate conclusions and beliefs, other people's opinions and limitations in my understanding had kept me bound for far too long.

We are not meant to carry the weight of our past experiences. Every human has experienced some level of past trauma. We all live in a broken and fallen world infiltrated by Satan and his demonic forces, principalities and powers.

"Cast all your anxiety on him because he cares for you."

1 Peter 5:7

"Look straight ahead and fix your eyes on what lies before you.

Mark out a straight path for your feet; stay on a safe path.

Don't get sidetracked; keep your feet from following evil."

Proverbs 5:25- 27

I have learned so much through adversity. Instead of accepting and believing everything that came my way, I discovered that I had a free will to accept or reject my thoughts. My thoughts create my reality. I am what I think. Not only are we told to take every thought captive and MAKE it obedient to Christ, but we are also told to let God transform us into a new person by changing the way we THINK. (Romans 12: 2) In addition, the helmet of salvation as mentioned in Ephesians 6:17 became an important part of my spiritual armor. The purpose of the helmet is to protect our minds from bombarding thoughts and desires, as well as the trappings and snares of the enemy. When I put on my helmet of salvation, I am guarding my mind in Christ Jesus. I might not be able to control what thoughts enter my mind but I can control whether to act on them or believe them or not. I can choose to respond or not respond and I can choose to accept or reject a thought, whether my own or someone else's. I am learning that I can control my habitual negative thinking patterns and I can reject the thoughts of other people if they are inconsistent with truth and God's thoughts toward me.

Instead of focusing on the sins or mistakes of my past and desiring responses to all the questions I could never ask from people who were unapproachable to me, I started asking myself some more important questions. What is my life producing? What do I want to accomplish with my life? What thoughts do I choose to invest in? How do I want to influence my family / community? How can I improve and strengthen my marriage? How can I develop deeper relationships and connections? How can I be giving more? How am

I serving God and others? I will give an account of my life one day.

I can live for myself or I can live for others. My goal must always

be to make an impact and live for something greater than myself.

Not for my glory, but for the glory of God.

Labels have only served to hinder my growth and I have

seen it as a stumbling block to so many. It seems as if we have

become complacent as Christians, seemingly unaware of the power

we have access to. Just like in the secular world, it seems as if we

have allowed labels to become our identifiers. My identity is in the

righteousness of Jesus Christ and in the power of His resurrection.

Being crucified with Christ means I identify as dead to sin and alive

in Christ and the life I now live, I live in Him through the power of

the Holy Spirit.

"Satan knows your name but calls you by your sin.

God knows your sin but calls you by your name."

Author unknown

Most of us have experienced abandonment, rejection and

betrayal in some form or another. Thankfully we are all in great company. What a comfort to know that even Jesus, in divine

perfection, came to his own people and they rejected him.

"Your approval means nothing to me,

because I know you don't have God's love within you.

For I have come to you in my Father's name

and you have rejected me."

John 5: 41

Chapter 14 - Purpose in Suffering

"To this you were called, because Christ suffered for you,

leaving you an example that you should follow in His steps."

1 Peter 2:21

Oysters can teach us a lot about suffering. Did you know that an oyster that has not been wounded in any way cannot produce a pearl? Apparently God created oysters with a shiny substance called nacre. The production of this material is a natural event that takes place when a painful foreign substance such as a grain of sand or a parasite enters the oysters shell. The nacre cells work to cover the source creating the pain with layers and layers as a protective mechanism. It could be said then that pearls are a product of pain. Like the oyster, our greatest ministry can come from our greatest and deepest wounds. Our pain can make us bitter or make us better. Our suffering definitely gives us reason and opportunity to grow and develop personal ministries of great value in serving others.

It never occurred to me, until I heard a speaker from a REFRESH TO CONNECT support seminar share, that as foster / adoptive parents we are fulfilling the law of Christ. (Galatians 6:2) The message in the overall theme of the conference, "We have been called to suffer for the redemption of another soul", felt like a precious healing balm to my hurting, wounded soul! "Oh Lord, do you really mean that all this pain and suffering is for a greater purpose and that purpose is the greatest purpose of all?" My heart overflowed at the realization that all "T.H.I.S." was not in vain! This pain, this suffering, this misunderstanding, this injustice, this lack of support, loss of relationships, this giving up of all financial resources... Other than for the love of God and the unconditional love for a child we'd never met.... I cannot comprehend what other possible reasons there could be to go through all the work and the waiting and the intense personal scrutiny and testing of every kind.

Just knowing God has a greater purpose beyond ourselves for our suffering makes it easier to not just take it up, but to embrace every cross and bear it. We become more like Jesus as we fellowship with Him through suffering. (Philippians 3:10) When I gained a deeper understanding of what Jesus endured on the cross and how He sacrificed himself for our greater good, I found it easier to yield to it rather than fight against enduring for the sake of others.

I began to understand that growing closer to God is not the result of trying harder but of surrendering more. During Calum's adoption, a precious sister in Christ shared an analogy of how God wants us to freely give so we can freely receive from Him. She explained how if we hold onto things with clenched fists, it makes it impossible to receive what God wants to freely pour into us. She explained that when we let go of "our" plans, perspectives, desires, etc. and open our hands with outstretched arms, we are in a position to receive God's best for us. Daily in my prayer times I would literally stretch out my arms, extended into the air with both palms of my hands open and literally give it all to Him; the outcomes, the trials, the victories, the challenges, the disappointments, every decision, every doubt, I frequently continued to give it ALL to God believing and knowing His plan was best.

Viktor Frankl was a Jewish-Austrian psychiatrist who authored several books. As a holocaust survivor, he had a serious encounter with suffering. His horrendous experiences as a prisoner in concentration camps during World War II were unimaginable, yet he somehow survived these tremendous horrors. To the credit of his ability to accept his suffering, he survived when those around him did not. In his book, he describes his experiences in suffering from starvation, frostbite, illness, and the loss of several family and friends. Although he was not a Christian, Frankl understood something invaluable about suffering. I appreciate the message he shares in his book;

" ... *the mental reactions of the inmates of a concentration camp must seem more to us than the mere expression of certain physical and sociological conditions. Even though conditions such as lack of sleep, insufficient food and various mental stresses may suggest that the inmates were bound to react in certain ways, in the final analysis it becomes clear that the sort of person the prisoner became was the result of*

an inner decision, and not the result of camp influences

alone. Fundamentally, therefore, any man can, even under

such circumstances, decide what shall become of him-

mentally and spiritually. He may retain his human dignity

even in a concentration camp. Dostoevsky said once, "There

is only one thing that I dread: not to be worthy of my

sufferings." These words frequently came to my mind after I

became acquainted with those martyrs whose behavior in

camp, whose suffering and death, bore witness to the fact

that the last inner freedom cannot be lost. It can be said that

they are worthy of their sufferings; the way they bore their

suffering was a genuine inner achievement. It is this

spiritual freedom-which cannot be taken away- that makes

life meaningful and purposeful."

(Man's Search for Meaning, Viktor Frankl, page 33)

Although I hate to see anyone suffer, I will be forever

grateful for the visual expression of Olga's pain which became the

precursor for a cascade of events that brought ten children into our lives and brought numerous opportunities for God's name to be glorified through sharing what He had done in and through our family. God always has a purpose for our pain. We can find assurance in our afflictions knowing that God has a reason and it is always for our good. As my trials and sorrows grew over the years, I discovered a greater dependency upon and a greater under-standing of my need for Jesus. Most seasoned Christians can testify to this truth as well.

"Through suffering,

our bodies continue to share in the death of Jesus

so that the life of Jesus may also be seen in our bodies."

2 Corinthians 4:10

Chapter 15

Sometimes God Sends a Dove

"And Jesus, when He was baptized,

went straightway out of the water

and lo, the heavens were opened unto Him,

and He saw the Spirit of God

descending like a dove and lighting upon Him."

Matthew 3:16

Doves are widely known as symbols of reconciliation, peace, love and forgiveness. At the time of Jesus' baptism, the Holy Spirit descended upon Jesus in the form of a dove as God the Father spoke to Him from heaven; "This is my Son, whom I love; with Him I am well pleased."

In a recent episode of The Chosen, Mary Magdalene was in a sentimental scene with Matthew as he described to her a divine meeting he had with a stranger who had gifted him an unexpected, valuable treasure. My heart immediately resonated with her line in response to Matthew's story: "Sometimes, God sends a dove." Yes! God can and He does send "a dove" at just the right time to encourage us or speak a word into our lives! He has sent many of these precious "doves" into my life at just the right appropriate times in addition to our blessing, Calum, aka "Dove- Messenger of Peace". In my experience, doves have served as affirmations of His love and presence in my life on numerous occasions.

As fall was approaching and the leaves were falling and turning their various vibrant colors, we traveled to southern Michigan one beautiful late September day to attend my niece's wedding. After the ceremony and celebration, we stayed the night at a Hampton Inn hotel in Port Huron, Michigan with nine of our children. At this point in our spiritual journey we were under the headship/ leadership of a man who seemed to abuse his power of influence. We had been brainwashed into believing that there really

weren't any excuses for not being in church when the doors were

open. So this particular Sunday morning, I struggled with the idea of

getting eight young children ready for church and then making the

three hour drive to get to church on time. It seemed nearly

impossible. In spite of my overwhelming guilt, we took the children

down for a continental breakfast and began the task of making sure

all the children got what they wanted to eat and drink. As usual, it

was obvious we were being watched. We had grown accustomed to

the curious stares of people who recognized something quite unique

about our family. We smiled politely in return. Over the years we

had also grown accustomed to the bombardment of questions: "Are

they all yours?" "Are they all siblings?" "Are any of them biological

siblings?" "Are they foster children?" "Do they speak English?"

"Where are they from?" But this day, we were about to meet a

couple that took a much deeper interest in all of us. It was almost as

if they had read the same "Experiencing God" book that I had read

several years prior. They seemed to recognize that God was a big

part of this story. They seemed to sense that He had been working in

and through our family, and they decided to "join Him". It was amazing and humbling to me how they recognized and articulated

that they had witnessed the love of Christ flowing out of us as we

related to the children. There was a depth to their curiosity that I had

not experienced before. They seemed to bypass the normal

questions we were accustomed to answering and seemed to

recognize God at work. They spoke into my life that day as I was

suffering from false guilt for not being in church that morning. They

challenged me to consider God's Word from Matthew18:20: "For

where two or three are gathered together in my name, there I am

among them."

Our new friends from Texas assured us that "In His name", we were

fellowshipping and worshiping God right there in the lobby of that

Hampton Inn hotel! The burden I carried all that morning for not

being in church that day was suddenly lifted.

My new- to- me sister in Christ, asked me if I was familiar

with the testimony of George Mueller. She had been rereading his

autobiography on their trip. She explained how he was an 18th

century Pastor from England who had taken in and cared for

thousands of orphans by faith alone, asking God only for the

resources to support his work. I was quite intrigued by this person I had never heard of. She later sent me that autobiography and I read it with great interest. I could easily relate to Mueller's passion for orphans, his trust and faith in seeking God for every need and in pursuing God through the work he had been inspired to do.

We shared our mutual love for the Lord, exchanged email addresses and reluctantly parted ways. I felt a connection to these special people who were obviously not nominal Christians, but sincerely active, practicing saints who had a living relationship with Jesus Christ. We had met this wonderful brother and sister in Christ not by accident, but by divine appointment! It later occurred to me it was all because we did NOT go to church that day.

Through many consistent phone calls and emails, I truly enjoyed getting to know our new friends in Christ. They possessed the wisdom of seasoned Christians who had been following after Christ for many years and they became like mentors for Todd and me. Over the next ten years, we became very good friends and we have received love and an abundant level of support in every conceivable way you can imagine from them. As they would always say, it was all for the glory of God.

One hot August summer day, not long after we moved here to Cadillac, Michigan we were attending a Christian gathering of worship at a park by a popular lake in our community. I had been quite upset and feeling like a terrible failure as a mother over some relationship issues at the time with one of our adult children. A well-known Pastor in our area, not yet known to us, came over to introduce himself. I could not believe his words of encouragement that seemed to come straight from the heart of God as he approached us. "You are doing a great job!" he said, with a bigger than life kind of smile and a twinkle in his eye. My usual response would have been a casual, "Thank you", but this particular day, I had to ask him: " What makes you think so?" (I was in shock over his timely words and desperately wanted to know why he said what he did.) He answered, "Look at their faces...", as he glanced and nodded toward the countenances of the eight children gathered all around me. "They are smiling!" Pastor Will could not have known the anguish of my heart, or what assurance I desperately needed to hear but obviously God did and He used Pastor Will to speak directly into my life that day. Pastor Will has become a great supporter and cheerleader for our family as we seemed to frequently run into him here and there and all around our new hometown. He always greets

us with a hug or a big smile and just seems to know how to

effectively love on people throughout our community.

Recently, one Sunday morning, a beautiful friendly lady from

church quietly stole a seat beside me just before the service started

and handed me an envelope with an instruction, "You can open this

later." I didn't think much of it since I too had been passing

Christmas cards around before church. As she suggested, I later

opened her Christmas card and out fell a folded letter and a check.

As in the faith and spirit of George Mueller, I had not asked for nor

explained our specific need at the time to anyone. I simply prayed

and actually repented, asking God for forgiveness because I felt that

I had allowed my peace to be hindered by our current financial

circumstances. I was feeling stretched by some accumulating

medical bills. First I read the note that had been written in her card.

I could hardly believe the exact words she had chosen to write as I

read her message. "A couple of weeks ago God laid you on my

heart to pray for you. Now He has touched me with a way to bless

you - especially at Christmas time. Please use this gift to help your

peace level - financial peace that is - to be at a good level. I'm sure with so many children you'll have ways to use it." She did not even

hardly know me and she certainly had no knowledge of my most

recent intimate prayers and concerns. I rejoiced once again for what

seems like a continual financial struggle as we have seen God's

faithfulness to provide for us over and over and over again.

I had noticed Mari at church many times before I actually

met her. I had often noticed her praying with or for people in the

hallways, and people just seemed to gravitate to her. I had also seen

her downtown on several occasions in all kinds of weather, riding

along in her electric motorized wheelchair. I didn't know her or

anything about her but I somehow knew she was someone very

special and I looked forward to the day I might get to know her.

That special day came one Sunday after church. Mari sought me out

and began speaking into my life as if she had always known me. My

heart swelled with joy when she referred to me simply as "mom" and

told one of our girls that she wished I would adopt her too! "When I

see your family, it just reminds me of the Kingdom of God. I am

reminded of what heaven is going to look like with every nation,

tribe and tongue represented," she announced. I was quick to let her

know that our family was far from a representation of heaven but I could understand and appreciate what she meant. I felt comfortable

sharing with her that not all was well with our family relationships,

somehow believing she would be quicker to pray than to judge.

Mari has prayed daily fervent prayers for our family since she first

met me. I have since realized to a deeper extent just how truly

spiritual in nature our battles have been. There is a battle raging for

the souls of our children.

Not long ago, I received this unexpected message from a

friend of our second oldest daughter who just turned forty years old.

During her middle school and high school years Jill had spent a lot

of time with our daughter as a guest in our home. We have stayed

connected after all these years. I have always been so happy for the

life Jill has chosen. For the past twenty five years, she too has

always called me "mom". She did not come from a Christian family,

but apparently just like Olga, she picked up on something significant

while staying with us;

"You have been my mom since the day you welcomed me

into your home. You have impacted my life in so many ways

and I will always be thankful and grateful. I wish my kiddos

could be around you more, but I hope that time will come.

You introduced me to Jesus and now my kids are being raised in a Godly home and that means the world to me in these days! Tell dad and everyone we said Hi! and give hugs. We Love You."

I felt tremendously humbled, yet thrilled, to know that God had revealed Himself to Jill in spite of our imperfect influence. The irony in her precious testimony was especially powerful since our daughter, her friend and reason for her time spent at our home was now a professing atheist and had turned not only against God but also against us. Although it seems we have lost so much, God has blessed us with so much more.

Reggie, Chloe, Roman and Jill Peoples

We didn't know what to expect as we drove from Mexico into the United States after leaving our Belizean jungle abode. Our trailer full of personal belongings seemed to strum up quite a bit of concern and interest at the Belize / Mexico border. At the U.S. Customs and Border Port of Entry in Brownsville, Texas, the officer sorted through all eleven passports as he called out each of our names to identify who was who. From there, we were instructed to pull our twelve passenger van and 5' x 12' trailer into a large carport type building where they x-rayed the contents. We were asked to get out of our vehicle and sit on a wooden bench while our van and trailer glided effortlessly through the x-ray machine. One of the children caught a glimpse of the most beautiful pure white dove carefully perched on a rafter overhead in the corner of the building as if it were observing and watching over us. We praised the Lord for the visible sign of the Lord's presence there in that place as we experienced His calm assurance about our decision to return to the states. Sometimes, God sends a dove.

Chapter 16

Legacy of Faith and Forgiveness

"Faith shows the reality of what we hope for;

it is the evidence of things we cannot see." Hebrews 11:1

There's a Chinese aphorism that says, "The journey of a thousand miles begins with a single step." Other than our initial desire to accept Jesus' invitation to accept Him as our personal Savior, our first real steps of faith took place just over twenty-six years ago now. We took the chance and started believing in and for someone we couldn't see. It was an exciting time and it was a lonely time. While we trusted that God was leading, our faith sometimes wavered as we were never certain of the outcome while walking into many unknowns. Over the span of our 42 years of marriage, by faith we have adopted ten children of four different nationalities, we have lived in a Belizean jungle, we have traversed through several foreign countries, and we have journeyed over 40 years through our own spiritual pilgrimage. Never could I have dreamed or hoped that God would bless us in all these wonderful ways. Even the suffering has been a blessing as it forced us to grow closer in deeper dependence upon and in relationship to our loving Heavenly Father. We are an intercultural family, a beautiful tapestry woven together by God's own hand. My own limiting beliefs of my capabilities and my own personal feelings of "unworthiness" could have easily predetermined a different outcome of our stories, but God had a plan that was beyond my own comprehension. Walking into His plans meant getting past myself, my opinions, and the opinions of others.

True faith is always tested. We know that God wasn't after Isaac's life on Mt. Moriah. He wanted Abraham's heart. I am continuously reminded to never doubt in the dark what God has told me in the light. Sometimes situations and circumstances in our lives don't make sense because they are merely a piece of a much grander picture. The greatest thing that can happen, as we experience the trials God sends our way, is that we grow closer to our Father in dependence and become more like Jesus Christ. Oftentimes while praying through the difficulties of our last two adoptions, I was reminded that when God wanted to do a mighty work, He started by sending a baby: Moses, Isaac, Joseph, Samuel, John the Baptist, and Jesus Himself. God can use the weakest to defeat even the mightiest enemies. By faith, we all have work to do in living out God's purposes for our lives.

Since all these things have come to pass, and these stories are now being written and documented, I realize how presumptuous some of these accounts could be interpreted to be. I would dare to say I have grown in my understanding of faith since many of these stories took place, but truly God met me where I was at the time. I cringed when I recently heard a sermon by Dr. Voddie Bauchman. He was explaining about our misconception of "blind" faith and that that actually does not mean removing intellect and reason from our daily walk and ignoring the mental abilities God has given us in considering our steps. In spite of our ignorance in neglecting our "reasoning skills" through some of our journey, God was there. There seem to be fine lines everywhere, but I am certain that our experiences, blessings and even our trials have all been initiated and

inspired by God for the purpose of revealing His heart to us.   It

could be said that taking a leap of faith should not be a reason to

plunge into irrationality. I've learned the hard way not to presume

God will be there for me if I run blindly into a seemingly good

situation without spending much time in prayer seeking His will

above my own.

When my mother passed away ten years ago, I inherited that

black leather Bible with the large gold cross embossed on the front

that I used to dust on her bedroom dresser. Prior to her illness, she

had become quite active in church attendance and she had a deep

appreciation for Bible study and prayer. By her calm and peaceful

passing, and the life she lived in loving her family well before her

death, I am assured she had a living relationship with Jesus Christ. I

often think of my grandparents' legacy and of their investment in

praying for their children and grandchildren. May the effects of their

faithful prayers live on through their grandchildren's children and

beyond.

Whether pursuing Biblical truth and a church body we could

call family, moving our family to a foreign country, or adopting a child internationally, we had to fix our eyes on Jesus, acknowledge

His leading and move forward one step at a time by faith. It required

more than effort, it required a belief and a trust beyond our own

understanding, although the two were strongly and synonymously

intertwined. With every new revelation of truth, every successful

adoption experience, every move down a narrower path, we

detached more and more from the ways of this world. When we

committed to following God His way and not our way, we found that

our faith had become unconquerable in spite of everything the

accuser of the brethren sent our way.

Years into my adulthood, I came to understand and

empathize with my dad who felt such woundedness in his own life,

that he would unknowingly project it onto his own children. Over

time, I was able to forgive my dad and many others out of a

desperate desire for my own healing and a closer walk with the Lord.

I found Jesus to be bigger than all my past and present pain. I began

to acknowledge that I couldn't be forgiven for my own sins if I were

not willing to forgive those who had and were intentionally or

unintentionally hurting me. Jesus gave us a command to forgive

seventy times seven times. (Matthew 18:21-22) In my

understanding, that means over and over and over again, which means allowing myself to be vulnerable and willing to be hurt again and again and again.

> *"If you forgive others their trespasses,*
>
> *your heavenly Father will also forgive yours,*
>
> *but if you do not forgive others their trespasses,*
>
> *neither will your Father forgive your trespasses."*
>
> Matthew 6:14-15

I have grown to appreciate the value and the life God has produced in me. I have experienced a great deal of satisfaction in being a wife and a mother, a missionary, teacher, gardener, writer, and most importantly, living out my faith as a disciple of Jesus Christ. Probably one of the most destructive things I have done in my life was to believe someone else's opinion of me, but according to worldly standards, my dad was right. I really didn't amount to much. I am not wealthy and have never even had a desire to pursue or accumulate wealth. I am not famous and don't have any special skill sets that I'm notorious for. With Jesus as my example, I have chosen to live somewhat of a humble existence since I first came to understand that this world is not my eternal home. I'm just passing through. I feel no need to impress anyone and I know that my value and my worth are not determined by worldly possessions or worldly wisdom. I have been blessed to be a guest in the homes of multimillionaires and I have been a frequent visitor in the thatched roof, dirt floor huts of families living in third world countries. God does not show partiality and neither do I. (Acts 10:34) My love will know no bounds.

"Faith by itself isn't enough.

Unless it produces good deeds, it is dead and useless.

Now someone may argue some people have faith;

others have good deeds.

But I say, How can you show me your faith

if you don't have good deeds?

I will show you my faith by my good deeds.

You say you have faith, for you believe

that there is one God. Good for you!

Even the demons believe this and tremble in terror.

How foolish! Can't you see that faith without works is

useless?

Don't you remember that our ancestor Abraham

was shown to be right with God by his actions

when he offered his son Isaac on the altar?

It seems his faith and his actions worked together.

His actions made His faith complete."

James 2:17

By faith I have lived and attained all my most significant

dreams. I didn't get my dream family of twelve children, but God

blessed me with fourteen instead! I not only visited Liberia, West

Africa, but many other countries as well. While dating, Todd and I

had dreamed of designing and building a log home. We

accomplished that vision in 1990. In high school, I had dreamed of

and was preparing to become a teacher. That goal was accomplished

as I began homeschooling my own ten youngest children twenty two

years ago. I have so very much to be thankful for. I praise God for

every one of our stories; the good and the bad, and for the grace that

can turn pain into beautiful pearls to be worn and cherished for the

benefit of others who need to come to understand their value.

"When it comes to achieving your dream, your view of God makes a

crucial difference." The Power of One Thing, Dr. Randy Carlson,

pg. 162

"It is impossible to please God without faith.

Anyone who wants to come to Him must believe that God exists

and that He rewards those who sincerely seek Him."

Hebrews 11: 6

The Weaver Family 2016

Back Row Left to Right- Raven, Ian, Addie, Noah, Calum, Todd
Front Row Left to Right- Esther, Livia, Liam, Noreen, Jenaya, Grace
Missing - Courtney, Megan, Drew and Chad

Chapter 17

Called To Adopt

"Pure and genuine religion in the sight of God the Father means

caring for the orphans and widows in their distress

and refusing to let the world corrupt you."

James 1: 27

I understand, in a perfect world, adoption would not be

necessary. In a perfect world, families would not be forced to

surrender their children due to the circumstances of life such as

poverty or the death of one parent. In a perfect world, Jesus would

not have had to come to die to redeem us from our sin.

Unfortunately, we live in a fallen world and all humanity suffers due to the consequences of sin. I know it is God's desire to work

through His church to be a father to the fatherless, to embrace and

care for the destitute, the orphan and the widow. When we first

started adopting, it was important to me to adopt a child that had no

living parents, but soon I was educated as to how most children

become eligible for adoption. I really hadn't understood that most

children living in orphanages around the world are relinquished and

/or abandoned by one or both living parents due to their inability to

parent or support their children. As children of God, we are all

called to fill in the gap according to His good purposes and I realize

that adoption is just one such way of doing this. We have supported

orphans and widows through sponsorship and facilitated

sponsorships and adoptions in several countries around the world in

addition to bringing children into our own family.

"Whatever you do, work at it with all your heart,
as working for the Lord and not for men." Colossians 3:23

I am thankful that our own adopted children understand the

circumstances that determined the decisions that were made on their behalf even though they had no voice to consent. They say a picture paints a thousand words. As I look at some of the photos that I have selected for this book, putting my personal influence aside, bad or good, I can see that God has made incredible life changing differences in the lives of our children. I am honored and thankful that He allowed me to be a part of their lives. The privilege of being called their mother is not lost on me. I am well aware that there are millions of other women in this world who could have easily been chosen for the blessing of this opportunity. God knew I was not going to measure up perfectly to the task, yet in my weakness, His grace has been sufficient. My continual prayer has always been that our children will all live a completely surrendered life to Christ and honor God in every aspect of their lives as they look to Jesus who is the author and the perfector of their faith.

Through Calum's adoption I finally realized why the negative and unthoughtful comments by those opposing our adoptions had always made me so angry, hurt and frustrated. Why did I care so much about what they thought and said? I realized that the most painful part wasn't that they were opposing us personally so much as that they were opposing God's calling on our lives.

When Jesus said to Peter, "Get thee behind me Satan," it was because he was attempting to hinder the Father's work. "Thou savourest not the things that be of God." He rebuked Peter, saying in other words, "Get behind me! You are doing the work of Satan, the adversary, in tempting me to violate my Father's command, and my undertaking, and to forsake the work God has for me." Maybe Jesus was frustrated too when one of his very closest friends didn't understand His purpose or His calling in going to the cross.

So many times I wanted to cry, as our children came to us with comments they had heard other adults from our church talking about their parents; "How old are Todd and Noreen? That just isn't right!" Like Peter, they apparently didn't understand or see the bigger picture. It didn't make sense to them, and they would never consider it. Therefore in their understanding, it wasn't the right thing for us to be doing.

They say adoption is not for the faint at heart. I would agree. The prayer life of a Christian adoptive family takes on a whole new intensity. Whatever doubts and concerns friends and family may have had, we had many more that needed to be worked through and addressed in continuous, fervent prayer. No one could ever know the questions that spilled forth from my heart night after night while we prayed for Calum's destiny. I surely wanted what was best for him and only God knew the answer to that. "Are you sure God? Are you sure that I can do this? At my age?" In the quietness of my prayer closet, my heart and mind wrestled with all the unknowns. I determined in my mind that this decision was God's to make. I would just make myself available to Him and pray, "Thy Will Be Done." I prayed many prayers of submission and surrender, asking God to determine which family He wanted this child to be raised in and resolved in my heart that I would be at peace with His decision.

Had God not chosen me and adopted me into HIS family, I'm sure my life would have taken a much different path. There probably would not have been any desire to live for anything or anyone beyond myself. I never would have known the love of our Heavenly Father who cares so deeply for the widows, the poor, the orphans, the destitute and even for people like me, whose value was questionable by my own earthly father.

I can't count how many people have asked if we are done. It sometimes comes with a smirk or an obvious look or sound of disapproval over our number of children. Coming from a very different perspective, I can't help but wonder, are they asking if we are done receiving blessings from the Lord? Are we done walking by faith? Are we done raising children for the Lord? Are we done believing God for the impossible? Are we done experiencing God and joining Him where He is working? I certainly hope not. Without challenging their meaning, I usually give them the answer they seem to be looking for and tell them that "Yes, Liam will be our forever baby. Yes, fourteen is enough."

God's love knows no limitations. To reveal this truth in my life and to others who know us, God gave us children of four different nationalities with varying skin tones and TWO newborn infants in our old age. No, not racial prejudices, not advancing age, nor persecution can keep us from sharing the love of Christ. His love knows no boundaries and He is not limited by short sighted personal beliefs and distorted perspectives of fallible, fallen men. Sometimes we tend to forget that love originates from God. God IS love. When we walk in His Spirit, His love flows freely through us without any constraint despite our many imperfections and personal inabilities, despite the limits we may put on ourselves and others.

"...Christ will make his home in your hearts as you trust in Him. Your roots will grow down into God's love and keep you strong. And may you have the power to understand, as all God's people should, how wide, how long, how high, and how deep His love is. May you experience the love of Christ, though it is too great to understand fully. Then you will be made complete with all the fullness of life and power that comes from God." Ephesians 3:17-19

In spite of us, God has helped our children overcome many obstacles and allowed them to grow up to be wonderful parents, respectful citizens of society, workers who are always applauded by their employers as having a wonderful work ethic, and most importantly, some have become missionaries and ministers of the Gospel. Just maybe Pastor Will was right. If you want to gauge a successful outcome, you have to look at the countenance of the fruit produced.

If you sense God stirring your heart, may He guide you, lead you, direct your path and make every provision for your journey is my prayer for you! He has done it for us therefore I trust He will do it for anyone whom He calls to serve in this way! There's a child out there that needs to know the LOVE of Jesus through YOU!

May these testimonies not only encourage you but also inspire you
to love without bounds.

"Love is patient and kind.
Love is not jealous or boastful or proud or rude.
It does not demand its own way.
It is not irritable, and it keeps no record of being wronged.
It does not rejoice about injustice
but rejoices whenever the truth wins out.
Love never gives up, never loses faith, it is always hopeful,
and endures through every circumstance."
1 Corinthians 13: 4-7

Feel free to contact Noreen at mom12gram7@yahoo.com

Adoption Resources

If you, or someone you know, are considering adoption I have briefly outlined the process and included some additional information to help you understand the process. The first and most important step in every adoption journey is finding a reputable agency that can provide your home study. A home study performed by a licensed social worker through an adoption agency is required for every adoption. It can seem quite overwhelming and intimidating at first, but your social worker will walk you through the process one step at a time.

There are three main components of a home study:

- The inspection of your home

- Interviews of all the people living in your home

- Gathering of necessary documentation

Local Adoption Agencies:

- Families Through Adoption
  354 Norwood Ave SE
  Grand Rapids, MI 49506
  1-616-242-9696

- Adoption Option
  4008 W. Wackerly Rd. #102
  Midland, MI 48640
  1-989-839-0534

There are three main avenues to consider if you are feeling called to adopt a child. There are pros and cons for each, so the decision is usually determined by each family's circumstances, abilities and / or desires.

International Adoption:

In adopting from another country, it pays to do some research. There are many things to consider. Every country has different requirements, so it's important to know what will be expected. Below are listed some reputable agencies that deal with international adoptions. They will explain which countries they work with. Most participating countries have special needs and waiting children programs. The average cost of international adoption is $30,000-$50,000.

- All God's Children International
  3308 NE Peerless Place
  Portland, OR 97402
  1-800- 214- 6719

- Bethany Christian Services
  1055 Carriage Hill Dr. #2
  Traverse City, MI 49686
  1-231-995-0870

- Holt International

1195 City View, P.O. Box 2880
Eugene, OR 97402
1-800-451-0732

Domestic Adoption:

In country adoption is one path you can take IF your desire is for a newborn infant. In most cases, you must create and submit a profile portfolio. A profile is sort of a scrapbook or photo book including photos and a letter introducing yourselves and your family to a potential birth mother. The more details you can include, the better, such as interests and hobbies and family vacation pictures, photos of your home and extended family members that you are close to and spend a lot of time with. Average cost is anywhere from $20,000-$45,000+.

Foster To Adopt:

Fostering to adopt requires prospective parents to go through several hours of training offered through your local public child welfare system. The main objective of fostering is usually providing temporary care until the biological parents can be prepared to successfully parent, but sometimes, the parent's rights are terminated. Therefore, the children then become available for

adoption. Fostering to adopt gives you a foot in the door so to speak.

Every state has different rules and fees.   Average cost is $0- $3,000.

"If you can't feed one hundred then just feed one."

(Mother Teresa)

Left to right: Ian, Raven, Livia, Addie, Noah

Left to right: Livia, Noah, Raven

Left to right: Esther, Ian, Livia, Raven, Addie, Noah

Back row: Raven, Ian, Addie, Noah.
Front row: Livia, Esther, Grace, Jenaya

Calum and Liam

Adoption is a deeper love than any natural love.

A more unique choice than any natural choice.

A richer gift than any natural gift.

A more fervent prayer than a natural prayer.

And something God did for all of us

Through Jesus!

(Author Unknown)

WEAVER, MY LOVE WILL KNOW NO BOUNDS

Currently, at the writing of this book:

1. **Adelyn** is finishing her teaching degree and pursuing a mission opportunity in South America. She has taught in Mennonite schools for four years and is currently a paraprofessional working primarily in the special education department. She is a voracious reader, and enjoys socializing with friends and collecting classic books.

2. **Grace** is working toward getting her license in Real Estate. She enjoys sewing and creating and selling her own all natural products.

3. **Noah** works independently doing home maintenance as a private contractor. He enjoys skateboarding, snowboarding and spending time with friends.

4. **Raven** works as a rehabilitation technician at a long term care facility for people with
neurological disabilities. She likes spending time with friends and has a deep love, respect, compassion and appreciation for children and adults with mental and physical impairments/ disabilities.

5. **Livia** is working with New Horizons Ministries in Canon City, Colorado. She enjoys painting, creative writing, cooking and baking.

6. **Jenaya** is a caregiver for children and works as a Nanny. She is currently pursuing a nursing degree. She lives in Ooltewah, Tennessee and enjoys traveling.

7. **Ian** works throughout the state of Michigan doing landscaping for road construction areas. He is an active hunter and avid snowboarder and is in the process of remodeling his home.

8. **Esther** is an Assistant Manager at our local GoodWill store. She volunteers with the youth ministry and serves in the pre-school department at our church. She enjoys decorating and planning special events.

9. **Calum** is a homeschool student, currently studying through second grade. He is active in AWANA, swimming, baseball and enjoys creating through various forms of art.

10. **Liam** is a homeschool student, studying through first grade. He is active in AWANA, swimming, and is a very talented basketball player.

I Would Gather Children

Some would gather money along the path of life,

Some would gather roses and rest from worldly strife;

But I would gather children from among the thorns of sin,

I would seek a golden curl and a freckled, toothless grin.

For money cannot enter in that land of endless day,

And roses that are gathered soon will wilt along the way.

But oh, the laughing children as I cross the sunset sea,

And the gates swing wide to heaven, I can take them in with me!

(Author unknown)

Sources and Recommended Reading

NLT Bible

Heavenly Man by Brother Yun

Living Water by Brother Yun

Suffering by Paul David Trip

The Connected Child by Karyn B. Purvis, David R. Cross

Humility & Absolute Surrender by Andrew Murray

Man's Search for Meaning by Viktor Frankl

Experiencing God by Henry Blackaby

Christ Esteem by Don Matza

Pilgrim's Progress by John Bunyon

Autobiography of George Mueller by George Mueller

The Power of One Thing by Dr. Randy Carlson

Emotionally Healthy Spirituality by Peter & Geri Scazzero

Dedication:

I would like to dedicate this book to my dad. He taught me more and made a greater impact on my life than any other person. He was a very cautious person who made parenting mistakes as a result of his unresolved childhood wounds just like I have. From him, I learned not to run with a sucker in my mouth. He taught me the value of "work before play". He showed me by his example the benefits of being tenacious. With nothing more than a sixth grade education, he literally made something out of nothing when he started his own successful business with the skills that he had. Every time I give a word of caution to my children, I can hear the echo of these same warnings that he once had given to me. Without the pain of living a less than perfect childhood I may not have attained all that I have. God truly causes everything to work together for the good of those who love him and are called according to his purpose. (Romans 8:28)

"O Israel, stay away from idols! I am the one who answers your

prayers and cares for you.

I am like a tree that is always green; all your fruit comes from me."

Let those who are wise understand these things,

Let those with discernment listen carefully.

The paths of the Lord are true and right, and righteous people live

by walking in them,

but in those paths sinners stumble and fall.

Hosea 14: 8-9

Made in the USA
Monee, IL
19 November 2023

46914964R00171